Table of Contents

Study Overview 1
Opening the Relationship 3
What Does Non-Monogamy Look Like? 8
    Joint vs Independent 9
    Disclosure & Integration 11
    Connection & Involvement. 15
Approaches to Rules and Norms 28
Typical Rules and Norms 33
Challenges and Difficulties. 38
What Helps 47
Couples' Sex Lives Together 55
What's the Impact? Benefits and Risks. 60
Discussion of Results 72
In Conclusion 75

Edition 1.03 — Date of release: February 21, 2010

Study Overview

Although non-monogamous relationships are very common in the gay community, little research has been conducted and information about how couples navigate this terrain is surprisingly lacking. As a long-term couple (34 years), this was a journey we had taken together, without a road map. The lessons we learned along the way were often hard-earned and we found ourselves wondering how others dealt with this. How common or peculiar was our experience? Were there models we hadn't considered? What worked or didn't work for others?

While recognizing the uniqueness of each relationship and assuming a wide diversity in approaches, we still imagined it would be valuable to hear from couples who had 'been there'. We initiated this study to hear directly from those couples.

Study goals

The purpose of the study was to better understand the experience of non-monogamous couples and glean valuable lessons. Study goals were:

- Gather basic information about how couples handled 'outside sex'
- Identify and describe typical models and approaches (to the extent they existed)
- Identify common themes, patterns, challenges and benefits
- Record what couples had to offer in terms of 'learning'

Participant selection

We chose to focus solely on non-monogamous couples. Although the similarities and differences between monogamous and non-monogamous couples interest us, we didn't feel we had the capacity or inclination to adequately investigate both.

Participants were recruited based on two criteria. Participants needed to:

- be in a long-term committed relationship (which we arbitrarily defined as 8+ years), and
- have some type of 'outside sex' or an agreement for such.

Recruitment was haphazard. We realized we had no way of methodically putting together a random sample or even recruiting a diverse population. We found participants by word-of-mouth, canvassing gay events (Pride, Folsom Faire, etc), and 'advertising' through articles and flyers in the gay press and gay venues.

Study population

As a result of our personal recruiting, we ended up with a majority of participants that looked like us – older, white, middle-class Americans - many from the Bay Area. In 19% of study couples, one or both partners were persons of color (primarily Latino or Asian).

The Bay Area was by far the most represented geography (35 couples). An additional 13 couples were from CA (outside the Bay Area). Other American couples were from FL (6), NY (5), NV (3), WA (3), IL (2), TX (2), CO (2), PA (2) and NE, TN, LA, HI, WI, DE. Nine couples resided outside the U.S.: Australia (2), UK (2), Canada (2), Mexico, Sweden and Netherlands.

Our population was also skewed in terms of age. Our youngest participant was 33 and our oldest was 81. Average age was 51. Surprisingly, almost 25% of the couples had significant differences in age. Seven couples had age differences of 20+ years and 13 additional couples had 10+ years difference in age. The average difference in age of all 86 couples was 7 years.

Partners had been coupled from 8 years to 42 years. The average length of time together was 16.2 years.

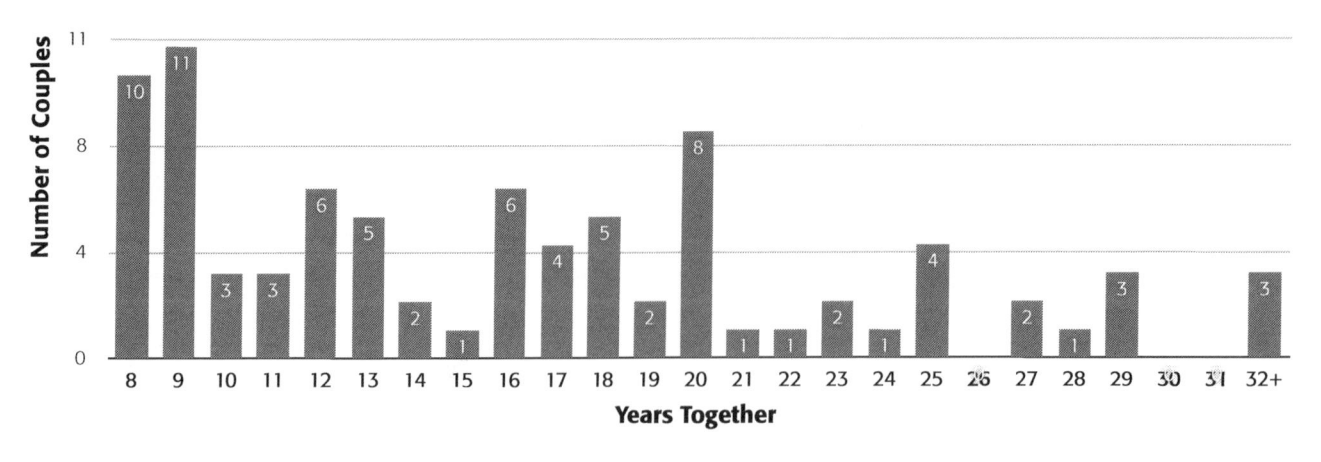

LENGTH OF TIME COUPLED

Average years coupled	16.2 years
Minimum length of time coupled	8 years
Maximum length of time coupled	42 years

Reluctance to participate

We found recruitment of participants difficult. We encountered a pronounced reluctance, resistance, or disinterest on the part of many 'eligible' couples for participation in such a study. We found long-term non-monogamous couples rather easily, but very few were willing to participate. Many declined immediately; some agreed, but didn't follow-through (probably typical in any study); and many reported back that their partner was unwilling. In a few instances, some couples got 'cold feet' (e.g. calling the morning of the interview to cancel; acknowledging the questions had raised unresolved issues, etc.). We can imagine all kinds of hypotheses for this reluctance, e.g. wanting to maintain privacy, lack of trust in us/the study, disinterest in the topic, as well as discomfort in talking about these issues.

Clearly our study population is not representative of all non-monogamous couples, but rather of couples secure enough to select into an interview process where they would be asked to openly focus on their relationship and the way they handle non-monogamy. Since we primarily wanted to find out what works, we figured this skewed us in the right direction – e.g. away from couples with deep unresolved conflicts, poor communication patterns, and horror stories of what doesn't work.

The interviews

86 couples participated. Each partner was interviewed separately using a consistent set of questions (see sidebar). Interviews lasted 45 – 60 minutes. 60% of the interviews were conducted in person. 40% of the interviews were conducted over the phone, (It helped that we had met 2/3 of these couples in person when recruiting). We chose not to record interviews (to protect confidentiality), but we took extensive notes and wrote a detailed summary report after each interview. Verbatim quotes were culled from the interview reports, to illustrate overall findings.

We also interviewed:
- The Center for Research on Gender and Sexuality, SFSU who have been conducting the Gay Couples Study for the last five years.
- 3 therapists who worked extensively with gay couples
- One man whose partner of 48 years was too disabled to participate
- One man whose who had lost his partner of 12 years to AIDS
- Three men whose partners ended up declining to participate

The study results, however, are based solely on the interviews conducted with the 86 couples.

Opening the Relationship

All of our couples by definition had agreement for some type of non-monogamy. Our first interview questions explored how that came about. As a starting point, we asked each partner to rate their inclination toward monogamy - when they first became a couple and currently. Results are below:

There were some obvious groupings:
- 36% were open from the beginning, with little change over time.
- 12% were slightly open and increased their openness over time
- 42% of couples were initially monogamous and opened their relationship considerably over time
- 4% were initially monogamous and opened their relationship slightly.
- 6% moved closer to monogamy and away from openness.

Surprisingly, we didn't find much difference in the 'current' rating of couples who were open from the beginning vs. couples who were monogamous at the beginning. If we only look at couples who began with an initial rating of 1 on the monogamy scale, we find their 'current' rating average at 6.2 (not much different than the 6.5 average of all couples). This would suggest that for couples who started out as open there is a fair amount of consistency over time. Their 'initial' and 'current' ratings were quite similar.

Although the couples who were initially monogamous all moved somewhat toward greater openness, five couples' who were open at the outset had moved closer toward monogamy. Explanations varied - they had consciously 'slowed things down', lost energy/interest as they aged, or felt more content with the sex they were having at home. This suggests it isn't always a one-way street. A few couples also reported that they closed their relationship from time to time.

> **Inclination Towards Non-Monogamy**
> **ON A SCALE OF 1 TO 10**
> (1=Fervent Monogamy; 10=Anything Goes)
>
> **All Study Couples**
> Initially – Average response = 3.5
> Currently – Average response = 6.5
>
> **Couples Starting as Monogamous**
> Initially – Average response = 1
> Currently Average response = 6.2

When relationships opened

We asked couples when they opened their relationships.
- 42% made an agreement to be open within the first 3 months, and by the end of the first year, 49% of all study couples had opened their relationship.
- The rest of the couples took from 1 year to 26 years to open their relationship – with the average being 6.6 years and the median 5 years.
- 10% of couples opened their relationship between year 1 and year 5.
- 17% of couples opened their relationship between year 5 and year 7.
- 24% of couples opened their relationship after year 7.

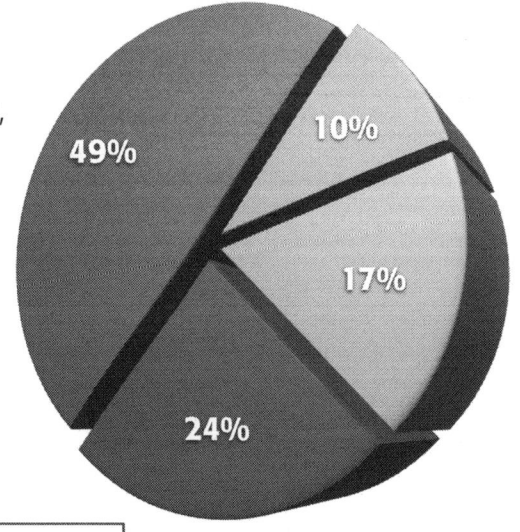

■ 49% within first year	■ 17% between years 5 and 7
■ 10% between years 1 and 5	■ 24% after year 7

Beyond Monogamy: Lessons from Long-Term Gay Male Couples in Non-Monogamous Relationships • Blake Spears and Lanz Lowen, Copyright 2010

Opening the Relationship

Understood from the Beginning

42% made an agreement to be open within the first 3 months of their relationship. Typically, these were couples where both individuals had a strong preference for being non-monogamous based on their own personalities and desires, and/or experiences in previous relationships.

> We went on our second date and Todd said 'By the way, if you're looking for monogamy, I'm not the guy.' I responded, "Oh, thank God!' Having sex outside the relationship has always been an option for us.

> Jerry's former boyfriend had carried on with a boyfriend on the side, so he was very clear that he didn't want to play games. We decided right up front. "I'm gay; you're gay; You play; I'll play. Let's be realistic and open about it". We were both on the same wavelength and wanted the same thing. I had been under lock and key in a previous relationship, so I was happy to be in an open relationship.

> Right after we met, I told Ted that I couldn't be monogamous even though I loved him. I just need another dick occasionally. Ted said, 'Great! I've found the man I want to be with!' We were definitely on the same page. We were open from the start, although we were mostly monogamous for the first 1 ½ years.

> We knew we both enjoyed sex with more than one person. We had to decide 'How is this going to be part of our lives?' We even considered having a period of monogamy to help build the foundation, but it didn't make sense to us. We were both coming out of difficult relationships and so we started couples counseling at the outset. We wanted to understand our own motivations and hear the other's. We decided we would always play together. There was no weirdness because we both liked seeing the other enjoy himself.

Took time to consider/discover

Some couples needed a number of years together before they felt comfortable moving to non-monogamy (average of 6.6 years before opening relationship). This gave them time to develop a trusting foundation.

> We were monogamous the first 5 years. For the first couple of years I don't think we ever even noticed anyone else. Then it took awhile before we got to the point of being able to acknowledge who we each found attractive. We talked about opening it up about a year before we did it. I think one of us was going on a trip alone – that became a catalyst to try it. We opened and closed the relationship a few times, depending on how we were feeling. It wasn't ever a big issue, but we've approached it cautiously and carefully.

> I think that as a hypothesis I was open to it from day one but realized that it took some time to feel totally comfortable about it and not feel threatened by Ken's interest in other men, especially if I felt they were younger, fitter, or sexier than me! When I felt sure of Ken, I could be less possessive.

> Eventually, there was one guy that we both liked and ended up doing a 3-way with. After that, we started talking more about opening the relationship, but I didn't know how to proceed. That was the beginning of our 'rule phase'. I was very surprised I ended up wanting an open relationship since it was different than my family's values and what I expected that I would want. It's funny – the guy we first did the 3-way with is now a good friend and we still do him occasionally

Pushing the envelope

In some cases, one partner insisted, advocated, cajoled or nudged the other in the direction of non-monogamy (14%).

When we got together, I sensed he wanted to be monogamous. He had been in other relationships and they were all monogamous. I had been in a five year relationship that was very open and that was my norm. We agreed we would be open, but he didn't really know what that meant or looked like or felt like. Two months into the relationship I happened to call him from the baths and he lost it. It was a big fight. I said if it's a deal breaker, then I'm willing to be monogamous. We decided we would be monogamous. About a year later, we were at a bar and someone hit on him and he asked me if we could take him home. We did and it was fine. For the next year, we did a lot of three-ways – we were Dallas's premier couple looking for a third. After the first year, I introduced him to the baths. We started going pretty regularly and for the first six months we always played together. At some point I suggested we be independent at the baths. He had concerns that this would be the beginning of the end of the relationship. Since then we've gotten in the norm of going to The Club every weekend and doing people separately. That's been our MO for the last 5 years.

It took us a couple of years. Terry insisted that we be monogamous, even though I wanted to play. Terry said that if we're going to move countries and give up a career, he insisted that we be monogamous in order to make that commitment. So we were monogamous for a couple of years. In Munich, we were in a leather bar and were being cruised, and I asked Terry if we could pick up the guy. Terry gave me an 'arctic look' that said absolutely not. It took another year or two before we opened it up.

We were monogamous until 4 years ago. I could probably still be quite content being monogamous. Ted decided, rather unilaterally, that he wanted to open the relationship. I initially had feelings of inadequacy and rejection. I suppose if I had said, "This is absolutely not acceptable", he wouldn't have done anything. But, I was also curious about what he wanted and wasn't getting at home.

Rex told me in the beginning that he couldn't and wouldn't be monogamous. I had a hard time with this the first 3-4 years. I talked to a lot of friends about it, and ultimately became comfortable with the arrangement. Being open allowed us both to fully experience what we wanted to. Rex always came back to me, which reinforced my decision to allow Rex total freedom. By putting Rex's needs first and following Rex's inclinations, I experienced things that I never would have on my own, and that's allowed me to grow in ways I never expected. I'm glad about that.

It just kind of happened

For some, it just seemed to show up quite organically as part of their evolution:

> Albert was propositioned. We went to a movie with the guy and then we talked about it all night. We went out with the guy again and this time went home with him. He was very respectful of our relationship. We were ready to have outside sex when this guy came along. It was a watershed moment to realize that we could be attracted to each other, but also have attraction toward others. It can be hard to say what you want.

> Four years into our relationship we were at the Gay Games and this guy started kissing Fred. I asked him if he wanted to invite him home. We did. Our friends were being very dishonest – saying they were monogamous, but then secretly going behind each others' backs. We wanted a relationship that was going to last. We spoke about it and decided to open it. Sex is sex; love is forever. It's an on-going discussion to some extent.

> It was a gradual process and continues to be negotiated. At year 5, we had a commitment ceremony and went on a honeymoon to Cancun and started to talk about becoming non-monogamous. Soon thereafter, we started playing with others when we were on vacation – it helped to be at ease, relaxed and far from home.

Getting caught / Coming clean

20% of study couples related periods of going out without prior agreement and having to come clean. Often the catalyst was a partner getting 'caught', followed by heated arguments and a traumatic owning up. This was not an approach any of these couples recommended.

> We never talked about monogamy. The first 7 years we were both trying to be monogamous (for the sake of the other), but neither of us succeeded. Nor did we acknowledge that we weren't succeeding. At 7 years, Luke and I were having very hot foreplay - I remember it clearly. The phone rang and it was someone Luke had been tricking with saying he had been exposed to an STD. I got angry and left the house. We fought about it, but soon realized we were both 'cheating' and so it was hard to blame the other. I quickly realized, "I love you and you're the man I want to be with". We decided we could be open and moved on.

> About 3-4 years ago, I walked in on Julian having sex with someone. We had a big fight and realized we both had been fooling around on the side all along. We had sex at the gym in the sauna or I occasionally met someone at the gym and would go to their house. It wasn't like either of us had affairs, it was just fooling around. Well, we decided if that's what we needed, then we should be open about it. So now we mostly do three-ways, but it's fairly open.

> It was a hard decision. We only talked about it 7 or 8 years ago. We both played outside of the relationship before that, but we didn't talk about it. We each assumed the other was doing the same. The relationship began to break down (energy, time commitment to each other, feeling honest). We decided we wanted to deal with the fact the relationship was open, but do it honestly. We broke up for 11 mos. We saw a counselor the whole time. We both wanted to stay together, but we had to move the relationship to another level. The dilemma was, "How do we have an open relationship that is fair and honest and will work for both of us?" We realized that being able to go out sexually is a part of who we are and what we both want. I wouldn't be as happy without it. We needed to give each other some freedom.

We're still unresolved

In some cases (6%), couples can't fully resolve the issue of whether or not to open the relationship. This can result in on-going conflict:

Barrett

It's always been a thorny issue for us. When we first met, I asked Ben to be monogamous, primarily because it was 1982 and HIV-awareness was rising and I was concerned about either of us seroconverting. However, Ben was very insistent that he be allowed to have outside sex and I was somewhat passive about it at first. For years 1-20, we both went out. Ben tended to have anonymous sex. I tended to get emotionally involved which caused conflicts with Ben. We still have conflict about how to handle outside sex.

Ben

I wanted it open and Barret wanted it monogamous. Even today, Barret would like it to be closed. We spoke about it repeatedly, but never came to full agreement. Over the years, Barret had a lot of outside sex, but now he's not going out. I went to sex clubs and I still have fuck buddies. There has been on-going drama because it's never really been resolved.

Leonard

We were exclusive for a few years, but then we did 3-ways. We did that for maybe five years and then it sort of stopped. We weren't traveling as much, we gained weight, AIDS became a concern, and opportunities didn't present themselves. We then had about 10 years of monogamy, although we didn't talk about being monogamous. I did phone and cyber sex, but never actually hooked up with anyone. Then once when I was traveling, I decided to go out and kept doing this when I traveled. I didn't tell Gil, but I somehow assumed he knew. This period lasted another 10 years. About two years ago, it all came out and now we occasionally have 3 ways and we have an agreement that we can go out. But it still isn't totally resolved.

Gil

Initially we travelled together and did 3-ways together when they came up. That was fine with both of us. We then went through a period of health issues. During that time our sex life diminished, but I just assumed he didn't want sex because of what he was going through. I thought we were growing as a couple, but I finally put two and two together and confronted him. He owned up to playing around on trips and that he had been for quite a while. He thought I knew. His stance was "I have to do things on my own." And he definitely wanted to keep going out. We almost broke up and we went to couples counseling. We have surfaced the issues and right now the agreement is we both can go out, but it isn't resolved. We're still in the middle of it.

What does non-monogamy look like?

When we started the study, we were hoping we might discover clearly differentiated models so that a couple might review advantages and disadvantages and rationally select a somewhat 'tested' approach. Our naiveté was short-lived. Early into the interviews we realized that relationships and approaches to outside sex were more often than not, quite different from our own, and much more varied than we imagined.

People and relationships are unique and there is no road map for non-monogamy. A couple has to be willing to discover their own path. Not having a model can be confusing, but also freeing. The norms aren't written in stone, so each approach to non-monogamy is organic, emergent and often iconoclastic. It has to be in order to fit the couple as they join, grow, change, mature and evolve.

While recognizing the uniqueness of each couple and their approach, we weren't satisfied with "It's a diverse panoply." We found ourselves continuing to define specific clusters in an effort to map different approaches. However, as hard as we tried, we couldn't find a way to elegantly describe the diversity. We did, however, identify what we saw as core pieces of the puzzle.

- We found three key variables that inform the 'characteristic look' of each couples' approach:
- Do they play together or independently?
- What gets shared and brought back?
- How emotionally involved do they get?

Key Variables

Joint vs. Independent
- Play separately
- Play together and play separately
- Only play together

Disclosure & Integration
- Acknowledged, but kept out of sight
- Communicated – details included
- Brought back, discussed and integrated

Connection & Involvement
- Anonymous contacts
- Fuck buddies and friends
- Deep connections
- Outside emotional commitments

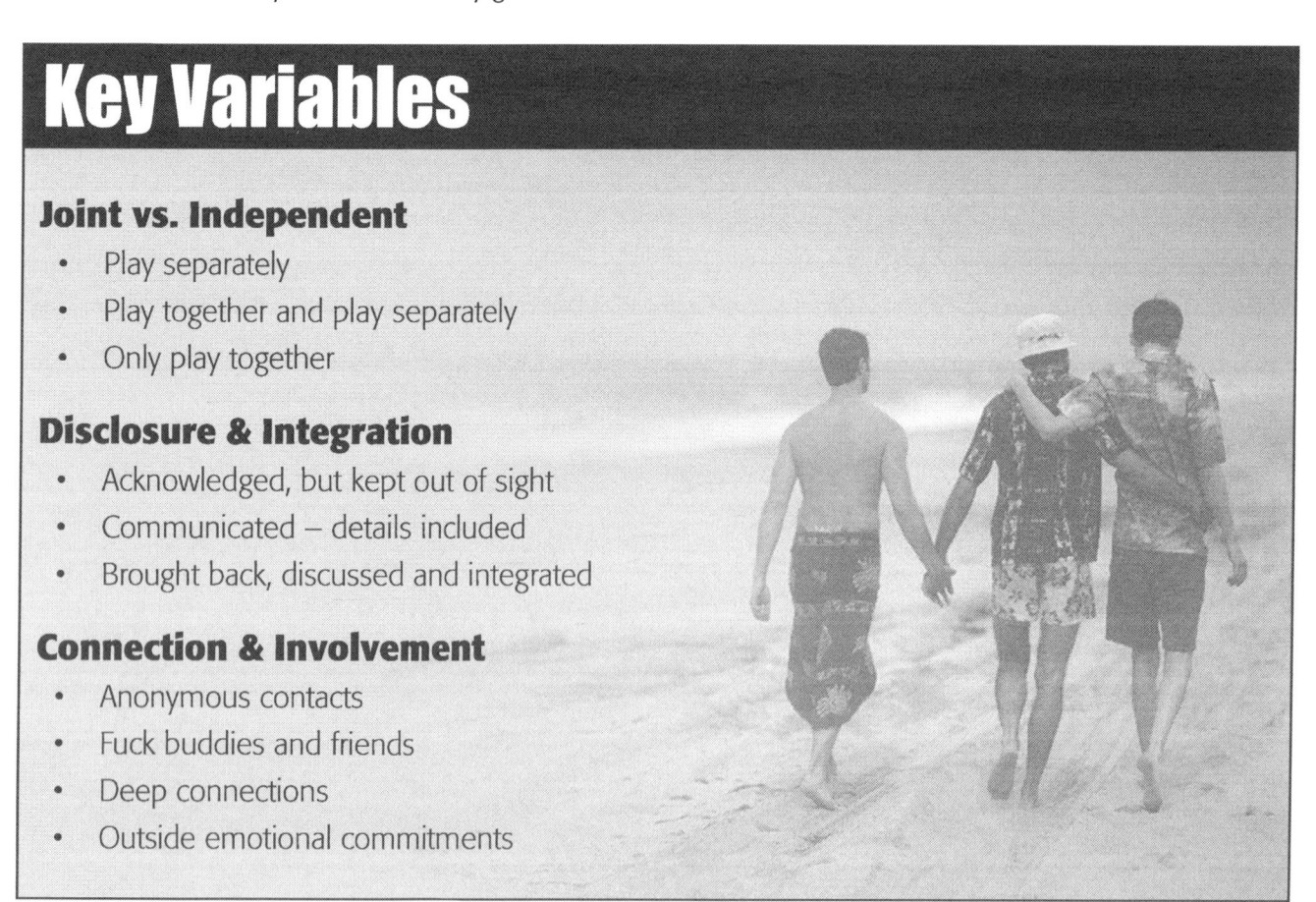

What does non-monogamy look like?
Joint vs Independent

The first variable is straightforward. Couples have to consciously decide whether they will play together and/or allow each other to play independently. Each has its advantages and disadvantages.

IF WE PLAY TOGETHER

ADVANTAGES
- We share the experience together, which could be enriching (and hopefully fun).
- It's reassuring since we're definitely clued in and have influence on how it transpires
- We can limit the opportunity for emotional involvement and unsafe sex (if we want)
- We have a say in who we do or don't do, when it happens or doesn't happen, etc.

POTENTIAL DISADVANTAGES
- We may have trouble finding 'outsiders' we both like or who like both of us
- We may get jealous, envious, competitive, and/or insecure
- We may not enjoy the same type of sex as our partner
- We may not get needs for freedom, differentiation, and self-growth met

IF WE PLAY INDEPENDENTLY

ADVANTAGES
- We get to have an experience separate from our partner where we're clearly the focus
- We have much greater control over who, what, when, how
- We can experience people or pleasures that may not be of interest to our partner
- We're not dependent on our partner's health, libido, willingness, desire for connection

POTENTIAL DISADVANTAGES
- We don't get to share the experience with our partner
- The onus is on us for how & what we report back
- We may be more likely to connect or get involved emotionally
- It could be threatening to one or both of us

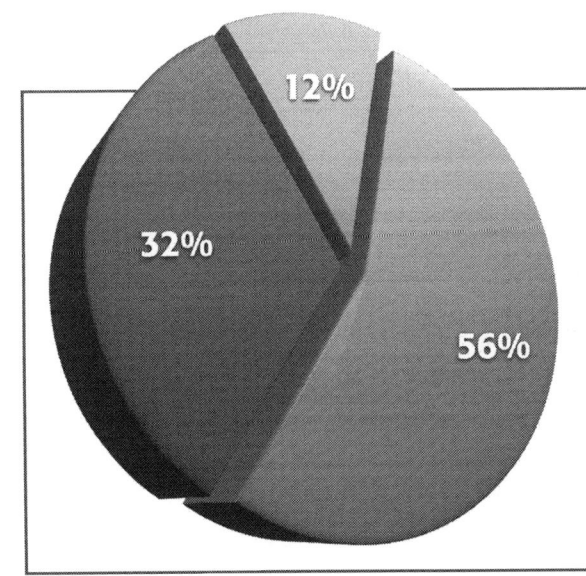

Study Couples: Joint vs. Independent

12% - of study couples chose to only play together (10 couples)
56% - of study couples chose to play together AND separately (48 couples)
32% - of study couples chose to play independently (28 couples out of 86)

31% - of the couples that did both, primarily played together and occasionally played independently

Beyond Monogamy: Lessons from Long-Term Gay Male Couples in Non-Monogamous Relationships • Blake Spears and Lanz Lowen, Copyright 2010

Consistency

Some couples chose an approach and consistently stuck with it for decades. This isn't surprising for couples who chose to play separately, but it also held true for some couples who decided to only play together. 50% of the study couples that only play together had been doing so since the beginning of their relationship – an average of 11 years.

Joint				Independent
Only play together	Play together unless at the same venue	Primarily play together & occasionally play separately	Play together and independently	Only play independently

Change over time

Many couples' approach evolved over time. The most typical pattern of change was couples who started by playing together and then gradually moved toward including independent play. This was often a result of the difficulty of finding appropriate 3-way partners and/or the increasing trust and comfort level that developed over time.

We didn't even acknowledge that we were attracted to other guys until 5 years into the relationship. 8 years into the relationship, we kind of impulsively decided to go into a sauna down the street. We did a 3-way with someone. We decided afterward not to do it again, but several weeks later we went back. For the next 5 years, we only went to saunas together. One day, David suggested we go our separate ways in the sauna. I didn't like that, so we didn't. But we have different tastes, so it's real hard to find someone we both find attractive. Eventually we started going to saunas and doing guys separately.

The terms have changed as we've changed. We started with trying 3-ways. The first guy was a zero, but we found the experience interesting. We continued in that mode (playing together) for awhile. I stepped out once and had overwhelming guilt. I told Terry and he was marvelous about it. We re-negotiated and for awhile had a 'get out of jail free' card. If something was too nice to pass up, we would call the other and use a 'get out of jail free' card. We did that for awhile, but it didn't really make sense – if you can't reach them it's a problem and so we let that go. Now we allow each other to play independently. We both wanted our sex lives to be fulfilling.

We had argued about monogamy at the beginning. I wanted an open relationship, but he said he would be pissed off if I was unfaithful. I knew I wasn't capable of monogamy. We decided we would only play with others together. Finding people that were equally attracted to both of us was difficult. We did find one guy we both really liked and he was very respectful of our relationship. We played with him for a couple of years. At one point I was traveling and ran into one of our 'joint tricks'. I made the decision to do him alone. When I told Dwight, he wasn't upset. This was the beginning of us evolving into having outside sex separately.

We started by playing in the backrooms when we lived in Europe. Initially, we played together, but then we started taking turns going to the back room. One would tend the drinks while the other played, but we always went home together. Over the years, it became okay to go home with someone and now we sometimes will hook up online when the other is out of town.

# What does non-monogamy look like?
Disclosure & Integration

The second key variable that has a big bearing on a couple's approach to non-monogamy is the degree to which information is shared and outside experiences are brought back to the relationship. If a couple only plays jointly, they share the experience as its happening. But for all other couples, choices are made on what to share and how outside experiences are brought back into the relationship. We saw a continuum between high and low disclosure and integration.

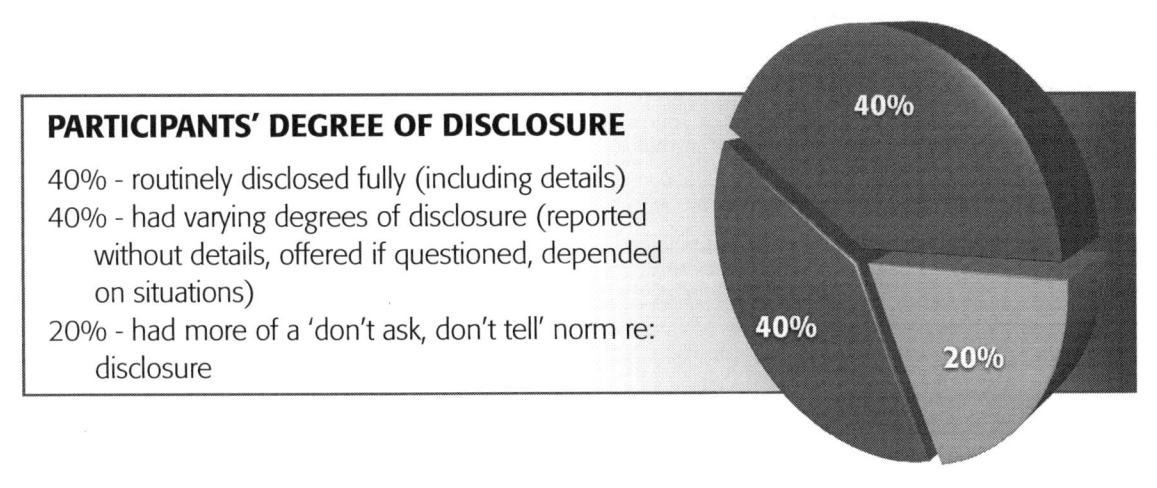

PARTICIPANTS' DEGREE OF DISCLOSURE

40% - routinely disclosed fully (including details)
40% - had varying degrees of disclosure (reported without details, offered if questioned, depended on situations)
20% - had more of a 'don't ask, don't tell' norm re: disclosure

Disclose fully

40% of study participants, who played separately, routinely report back, disclose details and share experiences. Some enjoy the process of reporting back and re-engaging. Some find knowing what happened reassuring. Some discuss the experience focusing on reactions and what it means to the couple's relationship.

> I was the more insecure one and I wanted rules. I needed to know what Wayne was doing. I didn't want to find out by surprise. I wanted him to tell me. That's still an important rule.

> We tell each other whatever we've done. It's not a rule. We like telling. I don't mind Pierce doing anyone, but it would hurt me if he deceived me.

> Everything gets shared. It's how I can be comfortable with the situation. I'd have issues if I didn't know about it. If it wasn't discussed, it might lead to emotional disengagement. Once you start closing down sharing in one area, it may creep up in other areas. I also enjoy hearing about what Cesar has done. It fuels my fantasies.

> If we split up at the baths, we share general info – Was it fun? What did he look like? Occasionally we introduce someone we've played with. We don't go into gory details or go on and on.

> Our first reaction when either of us meets someone we like is, "Oh, you've got to meet my partner". We try to integrate the experiences and outside relationships, rather than compartmentalize.

> There is a deeper level of honesty, trust and sharing. There aren't secrets. It's a learning experience I bring back to the relationship.

Show me what you learned

20% reported bringing back new sexual techniques and greater expertise. The experience not only gets integrated, but put to good use.

> It opens up sexual and physical ideas and options. We incorporate what we experience and learn into our own sexual repertoire.

> It's good to have sex with others. You see and experience something new and different. It gets brought back into the relationship when we talk about it. Often, when we share experiences, we say, "Mmmm, let's try that next time."

> Ted brings a lot of new ideas back. I like the variety. And it reminds us that others still find us both attractive.

> We share everything. When Jesse first started going out, he discovered that if he gave me details about what he did, then I would try those things on him. I learned a lot about what he likes and what pleases him.

> I've become a better cocksucker. Raul told me that and appreciated it.

Tell me again

The most commonly reported way of bringing back the experience was the sharing of details as a way of titillating each other. 35% of study couples described using the details to juice their own sex lives together.

> I usually want to know how big their dick was. We use it in foreplay.

> If Mac tells me and I'm titillated, then I'll ask more.

> It's fun to talk about the experience together. It's titillating. Even if we go out and don't pick up, the sex when we go home is very hot and fun. It adds an edge to the relationship. Graham's sex drive is diminishing and outside sex enhances it for us as a couple.

> I want to know. We talk about it. It helped me with my insecurity and it can enhance our own sex. I find it titillating. We also find out more about each other. "Is there anything else that he did you really liked?"

> We usually share – we find it titillating. I enjoy hearing after the fact. If I hear about it ahead of time, I get a little insecure.

Spare me the details

20% of study partners who played separately reported the encounter, but without sharing details. Another 10% said the degree to which they share depends on the situation. These couples may feel less of a need to share or may be less comfortable sharing. Some have learned how much their partner wants to hear and make choices accordingly. 10% have an agreement to only share if questioned.

> We both share details at times. It's often exciting, but it can cause a little jealousy. Sometimes I filter what I share based on who the other guy is. We like to compare notes, but we definitely try to not make the other person envious.

> If something funny happens, we share it, or if it's likely to be of interest to the other one. However, I like more kinky sex and Loren doesn't want to hear it, so I don't tell him that stuff. And Loren likes more 'traditional' sex, which bores me.

> I don't report back what I do. Hugh shares because he wants to share. He likes to talk about what happened. I'm not a jealous type. In fact, if he tells me, I get turned on.

> I share all the details although Ryan might not want to hear them. I like hearing the details from Ryan – I create fantasies based on his exploits. However, he usually just says that 'he went out' and doesn't elaborate.

> When we play apart, we acknowledge that it happened, but we don't' share a lot of detail. Neither of us needs to know a lot about the other's outside activities. However, if it was a good experience for one of us, and we want to repeat, then we will discuss it and perhaps even bring the other one along.

> There are some things that happen in the margins that don't get shared. There's an acceptance of unfaithfulness -that sounds harsher than I mean it - but we can read each other.

Finding the balance

A few couples talked about the difficulty they had in finding the optimum amount of information to share.

> We're still working out what we talk about. Cliff doesn't want to tell me what he does and doesn't want to hear what I did. I like sharing and the idea of not knowing what Cliff is doing is very unsettling; We've been in couples counseling the past year.

> It's been very hard for Patrick to be open about what he does sexually outside. I'm more open. Most of the change has been with Patrick becoming more open about what he shares.

> The hardest thing has been to know how much to talk about what we did outside. I tend to form relationships easier, and it can threaten George. It's harder for George to form relationships, so he sometimes sees me as being more invested in the outside relationship than I actually am. He views my relationships as more emotionally connected than I experience them.

> It's very hard for me to open up and talk about things. Talking about sex is difficult. We share most stuff – at least when it seems significant. But if he finds out later, even though I didn't think it was a big deal, then he feels like I'm not telling him everything. I doubt he tells me everything, but its okay with me.

> Tom wanting to always hear the details in order to get titillated got wearisome. I'm probably more promiscuous and I don't mind sharing some details, but it got to be too much. I had to tell him, "If you want me to be honest and tell you about what I'm doing, you can't always ask for all the little details". It begins to intrude on my own experience.

Fine distinctions

Some couples make fine distinctions about what needs to be reported:

> You have 3 days to divulge, but if it's not oral or anal it doesn't count as sex. Jacking off in the gym shower doesn't equal sex so there's no need to report.

> We do have what we call the "Sauna Clause". Basically, whatever happens at the gym, stays at the gym.

Don't ask, don't tell

At the end of the continuum are couples (20%) who agree to share very little. They have an understanding that outside sex is permitted, but generally not discussed. Some referred to this as "don't ask, don't tell".

> There are no explicit rules, but it's very limited. Any outside stuff has to happen by 6 pm because we spend all our evenings together. I guess we have the "Don't Ask; Don't Tell" policy. We don't discuss and we choose to be discreet.

> We have an agreement that it's okay to go out, but we generally don't report back. When Mack gets back in town, I don't tell him that I went out or who I played with. I suppose he could ask, but he never does.

> We still do 3 ways. We have a norm not to tell about anything else. I may see someone while he's traveling, but I don't tell him. It all feels insignificant, so it's easier not to tell him.

What does non-monogamy look like?
Connection & Involvement

The third key variable that shapes a couple's approach is the degree to which couples and partners are open to connection and emotional involvement. The continuum for this variable looks like the following:

Connection Limited				Involvement Permitted
Anonymous contacts	Fuck buddies	Friends with benefits	Deeper connections	Emotional commitments

Avoid connections

Many couples prefer anonymous contacts. 34% of our study couples avoided both emotional involvement and on-going connections (whether out of precaution or because of their preference for anonymous sex). Many tended to see sex as 'just sex' — quite separate from love or their relationship with their partner. For others, limiting connection with outside sex partners is a way of preventing emotional involvement, something they see as potentially threatening or problematic.

> We don't have an explicit restriction, but the norms we've created and the way we are each personally wired pretty much precludes emotional involvement. I can only love one man at a time and so I'm not emotionally available. I adore anonymous sex. We both have our tricks that we play with multiple times at the baths, but it's not more than that. It's, "Gee that was fun. I already have a commitment." Even when the sex is very good, I get bored after 2 or 3 times.

> Nothing stated, but we both firmly believe in sex as just a release. If it were emotional, it would be much more threatening and would feel like cheating. Even now, I have some guilt that I should be home rather than out looking for sex.

> We don't have any regular fuckbuddies and none of our tricks have become friends. There's a pretty strong distinction between meeting sexual needs and emotional needs. We're both men and there's that desire for variety. By being together when we play, it makes it safe/non-threatening. It's a built-in mechanism that allows us to blow off steam. We expect our emotional needs to be met with each other.

> We can schedule something with someone, but not a second time. It's not a problem if you happen to run into them again, but the point is you're not planning/setting things up and seeing someone repeatedly. We're not looking for emotional attachments and we don't want them. It's a hard and fast rule that avoids complications.

> It's not an issue. Sex is sex. I love Gil. Gil loves me. There is no outside emotional attachment — we're not looking, needing, or wanting.

ALL STUDY PARTICIPANTS:
- 34% - avoid connection - generally or exclusively have anonymous contacts

66% - prefer and/or permit some type of connection:
- 40% - typically have fuck buddies and/or friends with benefits
- 20% - have deeper connections – more than friends, but secondary to partner (includes 'above board' affairs and couples who take on temporary 'boys')
- have emotional commitments (triads, polyamorous families)

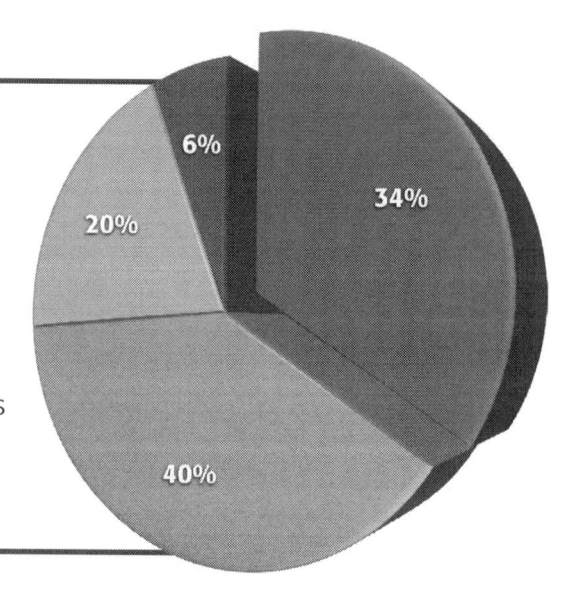

Connection allowed

A much larger group (66%) of study couples preferred or permitted some type of connection. Some couples kept the connections very limited and some couples allowed greater involvement. Connections (in order of increasing involvement) included:

- Fuckbuddies ("We only see each other for sex.")
- Friends with benefits ("We're friends, but occasionally we have sex.")
- Friends who've lost benefits ("We can continue the friendship, but not the sex")
- Friends of the couple ("We all get along and enjoy hanging out even though initially he was Tom's trick/friend.")
- Our boy ("We both love him, but not in the same way we love each other")
- Committed Third or Polyamorous Partners & Families

40% of participants typically have regular or occasional fuck buddies or friends with whom they have outside sex. 20% have deeper connections – These include 'managed' infatuations, 'above board' emotional involvements/affairs, partners or couples who take on a 'boy' or a 'third' for a period of time, and on-going long-distance relationships that are more than friendship, but secondary to the couples' relationship.

Connection allowed, but limited

For most couples, even when connection is allowed, there is a limit. 75% of study couples had rules or norms that precluded or limited involvement. Where a couple drew the line between what's okay and what's 'too involved' varied. It depended on:

- their values
- their expectations and desires as a couple
- their level of comfort with involvement
- their level of trust in each other
- to what degree the specific 'outsider' was perceived as a threat
- the norms they had developed

Connection allowed, but limited

We're so tight and bonded that there's no room for anyone else. There's not really a chance for someone to get involved emotionally. I'm the one that is more likely to get involved emotionally since I see guys repeatedly, but they know from the beginning I'm attached. I quickly distance myself if anyone starts to get clingy or too close emotionally.

We have a clear rule that we're supposed to stop if emotions are getting involved. It's happened with me once. I had to tell the guy, "No, I'm not going to tell you I love you."

I don't think we ever had to say, "Don't fall in love with someone". Emmanuel is into anonymous sex; I'm the one that would be more inclined to form relationships. There have been a couple of people who I had sex with who became friends and became our friends (and Emmanuel had sex with as well). It wasn't a problem. I don't think I ever got too involved. Instinctually, I might pull back if I was getting infatuated. But I never felt like I was holding myself back. I think it's more that my needs are being met by Emmanuel, my family and our friends.

Neither of us wants an emotional connection. We're free to make friends and get close, but my heart is and has always been with Byron. There is a boundary between love for a friend vs. my love for Byron. I had a boy that lived in Chicago. There was some emotional attachment, but it never crossed that boundary. I was more like his father. Byron had a couple of boys too. We liked being mentors – they were a lot younger and it gave us a role and we did it together. It added to our relationship. They ran their course and moved on.

Differing preferences for connection

One of the most striking study findings was the large percentage of couples (35%) where one partner preferred anonymous sex, while the other only enjoyed sex with friends or people with whom he felt connected.

Ted doesn't like to kiss, touch, caress. He likes wham/bam, to watch, and very anonymous encounters. I like getting to know the person and touching. I want foreplay.

Brent goes after everything, but I want to know someone before I would ever want to have sex with them. Yeah, once I guess I had a bit of crush. He was really cute and really nice. I stayed in touch, but was very careful in my correspondence so that I didn't encourage anything. It passed. I don't worry about intimacy with others. I would stop myself from it. Brent? Oh he's incapable of it (laughs).

I prefer having anonymous sex. If I know their name it can ruin the experience. I've seen a few guys several times, but I don't want to become attached or emotional. I have what's called "New England emotional shutdown" – if someone is feeling an emotion, we can have a piece of cake. Tim is wired differently. He falls in love and processes like a lesbian.

We're very different people. Anyone can suck my dick, but I only kiss someone I love. I would feel embarrassed kissing someone I didn't love. Dale is opposite. Dale wants to get to know them. I just want a blowjob on the way home from work.

I lead with my emotions. We used to say that I could have a close friendship that would be as threatening as Mel having sex. But Mel's not at all jealous. I feel no restraint from Mel to rein in my emotions. There's no leash, but I stay pretty close. I feel trusted and that makes me more secure of myself.

For Ted, "It's just sex." I'm much more of a romantic – I see sex as linked to romance. The bathhouses and sex clubs never worked for me. I'd rather know something about the person – then I'm more comfortable.

Chip

Barry is more emotionally focused than me. He gravitates toward regulars. It may be a transient relationship, but for that period they're very connected. I had a couple of guys who liked me, but when that happens I get very uncomfortable. Barry would love for me to be more connected to his 'regulars'.

Barry

For me sex is love. I like guys who are emotionally available, but only to a point that doesn't require I get involved in a way that would affect my relationship with Chip.

Where's the line? Managing involvement

Having one partner open to and preferring connection was not problematic for some couples. However, for many couples there was a learning curve for each partner. The partner who preferred anonymous sex had to grapple with: "How connected does my partner have to be and what impact will that have on me/us? Will he fall in love and leave me? Will I be okay meeting and possibly hanging out with friends with whom he's been sexual?"

The partner who preferred connection had to discern, "What is the line between connection and romantic involvement? Will I be able to stop myself at infatuation? How can I follow my heart, but not hurt my partner or jeopardize our relationship?" Many couples learned what worked for them without too much drama.

> I was concerned "Is he falling in love?" He reassured me. I met the guy a few times. I thought of the whole thing as Adam going thru a phase. I considered it more an annoyance than a threat. I've learned emotional involvement isn't as binary or clear cut as I thought it was.

> There are no restrictions. I'm the trouble-maker on this one. Art gives me tremendous leeway. I get close to friends and like to hang out with them, but it never makes me not want to come home to Art. And if I get close to someone, I'm always open to including Art - they're not exclusive friends.

> There's always that risk. There was one guy I started getting involved with so I stopped myself. There are no rules about it, but there's an understanding that our relationship is most important. Norman definitely got emotionally involved with Sam. He would just as soon have his tricks over for breakfast, but I'm not comfortable with that.

Lewis

We're primary to each other. We can depend on each other so unquestioningly. He's had a number of serious health issues and to be able to be a support to him has been really important to me (as well as to him). Walter is emotionally involved with Gene, and even I have an emotional connection with Gene. But it's very secondary to Walter's and my relationship. Our sexual relations with outsiders just aren't that important compared to our relationship.

Walter

I only enjoy sex with people I know and like. I love my friend Gene and he sometimes spends the night at our house. But I think of my relationship with Lewis as being emotionally monogamous.

Clark

Anonymous sex does nothing for me. I only get sexually aroused by people whom I know and have some connection with. So, I do get emotionally involved. It's been a minor issue a few times. . Most of our friends are people that I got involved with. Owen feels more threatened because I need more involvement. The sex usually quickly falls away and then we're usually friends, and Owen is close to almost all of them.

Owen

I don't take names or numbers. Clark gets emotionally involved and that can feel threatening. Early on, I got very insecure, but I've learned to trust Clark and the relationship. I realize I'm not in control, but I decided I have to trust that Clark and I have the same goals.

What helped couples navigate this terrain?
- Relying on their sense of trust
- Reassuring each other
- Exercising restraint
- Setting clear boundaries
- Integrating the 'outsider' into the couple's relationship (e.g. became joint friend)
- Limiting the sex if the involvement felt too threatening
- Ending the outside relationship if that was what either partner felt was needed

Going too far

While 75% of study couples had rules or norms that precluded or limited involvement, 15% with this norm had experienced finding 'the line' by going 'too far' and realizing they needed to pull back:

I fall in love. He calls it "emotional wandering" and puts his foot down. I cut it off totally, cut out the sex, or include Cliff in the sex.

We met a 34 y/o boy, Lucas, who Warren was strongly attracted to. I was attracted to him as a friend. Lucas ended up moving in with us and Warren and he had a strong sexual relationship. There was no jealousy, no drama, everyone was open. Our friends kept warning us. "What the fuck are you doing?" Their fears bothered me, but I had encouraged the situation. I was having anonymous sex and enjoying that and they were spending a lot of time bonding. Lucas lived with us for 1 ½ years, but Warren slept with me every night. I became the "Daddy" and they were the two boys. I liked that role. I felt left out and delighted. Warren's a lot of maintenance so it was a relief. We stayed the course until it was time to shift and we all agreed that Lucas needed to move out, although he's still family. We now have a different model. Warren has a handful of fuck buddies and I tell him he can have sex with whomever he wants, but he can't have dinner with them.

At first, Miles was quite carried away by Donald. It was very de-stabilizing and I drew the line. The three of us played together a few times and then we agreed that Donald would have dinner with us four or five times a week and the three of us would play once a week. We did this for a year and a half. Fortunately, Donald had a strong sense of fairness and he and Miles became much more aware of my needs. I now see it as a youthful infatuation on Miles's part.

Dating or emotional attachment would spell trouble – so we don't do it. I had one affair. We talked about it all the way through it. Bob handled it better than I did. I'm more promiscuous, but also the one that's more likely to get jealous. The affair lasted two months – it was with a married guy. At no time did it jeopardize my feelings for Bob. The guy was all over me telling me he loved me and when I finally gave in, he was gone. Bob was very supportive around my feelings of getting dumped. In the long-run, I lost my appetite for outside sex as a result of that experience. It certainly made me appreciate Bob more.

Daryle

Early on, we didn't see a person more than once. That's not the case now. Now we say "No affairs". Affair = emotional, erotic, sexual commitment that draws energy away from Elliot. We have the rule because I did have an affair at the 7 year point and it lasted 9 months. It was painful for everyone. Now, I'm much more careful to have 'friends with benefits.' If there's no romantic affair, no one gets hurt. It has been trial and error and it's still an issue.

Elliot

Daryle got emotionally involved, but now if he did, it probably would be okay because I trust that he won't leave me.

It helps if we both prefer connection

It may be a bit easier for couples where both partners favor connecting to their respective 'fuck buddies'. There's still a learning curve, but more opportunity to empathize and to join in discerning what feels appropriate and what feels 'over-the-line'.

The feeling of connection is what makes sex hot, so there is some emotional involvement. We've become friends with playmates and friends have become playmates. We both enjoy being open-hearted.

Mitch

We realize it's just sex and we save our emotions for each other. We never tell anyone else we love them - that's just for us. We have good strong feelings for our friends and fuckbuddies, but as friends. They know it's about the sex and they're respectful of our relationship.

Steven

It's never really been a problem. There were a few times very early in the relationship where I got infatuated, but Mitch called me on it and I backed off. I always look at it from Mitch's perspective — "How would I feel if Mitch did this to me?" For the two of us, the relationship is paramount.

Logan

We're very comfortable with the strength of our relationship and we're not worried about anyone taking either of us away — so there aren't any restrictions. However, we both expect to be primary. Friends or tricks could be emotionally involved, but they're more like satellites. We have crushes, but I don't allow it to go further. We understand the importance of our relationship. It's our bed I'm going to come home to.

Dwight

For myself, I'm careful not to let anything get out of hand. I learned in a previous relationship where to draw the line. I don't want to fuck up what we have.

Zak

There are no real restrictions. I have playmates I've played with for 2-3 years. Martin has met them. It's important for them to see that I have a partner. I make it very clear that I will be going home tonight. Single guys often want a relationship. I can't provide that, although they're welcome to come back to the well repeatedly. Sometimes, I have to be very clear, "That's not going to happen." I'm always quick to introduce Martin. If they get clingy, I pull away. During year two, we did have a 3rd in our relationship for about 6 months. He didn't live with us. He wanted me and we knew that, so we watched him. Martin was more suspicious than I was, but we made it clear to him. He realized the situation and moved on, although we're still friends.

Martin

They fall for Zak. Occasionally they have fallen for me, but usually with Zak because he's a social butterfly. We then have to navigate that. I don't tell him to stop seeing the person, but we talk and do confirm that they need to be reminded its physical and a friendship — not more. We let it play out, even if they're macho and think they're going to win Zak away. It's about them, not us. We don't want to lead them on or damage their self-esteem. They either get it and deal with it or they move on.

Larry

We don't have rules. We have run into only one situation. We had a visitor from Argentina – a young kid. I felt like an affectionate big brother. The three of us played - Dennis more than me. Dennis was aware I found the kid very appealing and we both knew the kid was going back to Argentina. But it turned out that Dennis felt uncomfortable and threatened. I felt warmly toward the kid and flattered that we had some type of bond, but it wasn't at all comparable to what I feel for Dennis and certainly not a threat. However, I wasn't being aware of how it might be impacting Dennis. There is a line. We do get close to some of our friends, but my feelings for Dennis are qualitatively and quantitatively different. One of the key things we believe – a third can't break a sound couple up. As long as we love each other, nothing will pull us apart.

Dennis

We're sometimes sexual with friends and some 3-ways have become our friends. We both know we're allowing ourselves to be open to others. To some degree, that puts the relationship 'at risk' but it makes us both feel free and that we're choosing to be in the relationship. Larry had a cute guy from Argentina visit and he told me how special the guy was. I felt threatened by that and told Larry my fears. Larry felt really bad that he had caused me to feel insecure.

Or is it double the trouble?

On the other hand, for some couples where both partners favor connecting with outsiders, there may be less vigilance and a tendency to allow more. Sometimes one or both go "too far".

I was concerned "Is he falling in love?" He reassured me. I met the guy a few times. I thought of the whole thing as Adam going thru a phase. I considered it more an annoyance than a threat. I've learned emotional involvement isn't as binary or clear cut as I thought it was.

There are no restrictions. I'm the trouble-maker on this one. Art gives me tremendous leeway. I get close to friends and like to hang out with them, but it never makes me not want to come home to Art. And if I get close to someone, I'm always open to including Art - they're not exclusive friends.

There's always that risk. There was one guy I started getting involved with so I stopped myself. There are no rules about it, but there's an understanding that our relationship is most important. Norman definitely got emotionally involved with Sam. He would just as soon have his tricks over for breakfast, but I'm not comfortable with that.

Lewis

We're primary to each other. We can depend on each other so unquestioningly. He's had a number of serious health issues and to be able to be a support to him has been really important to me (as well as to him). Walter is emotionally involved with Gene, and even I have an emotional connection with Gene. But it's very secondary to Walter's and my relationship. Our sexual relations with outsiders just aren't that important compared to our relationship.

Walter

I only enjoy sex with people I know and like. I love my friend Gene and he sometimes spends the night at our house. But I think of my relationship with Lewis as being emotionally monogamous.

Involvement permitted

A few study couples described situations where partners got very involved, but they were reluctant to squelch it. Even though it created tension or was potentially threatening, the partners preferred not to put constraints on each other. In these cases, everything was very transparent, discussed frequently and ultimately treated as learning opportunities

Wayne

Jim is seeing someone who he really likes and they have gone on two weekend excursions together. If there was ever going to be a threat, it's probably this guy. Jim is keeping me informed and I can tell by his demeanor that nothing between him and me has changed. He has sexual and spiritual needs I know I can't meet. He likes drugs and intense sex. I don't do either. I know my limitations and I've always been secure. It's about mutual happiness and mutual supportiveness. I'd rather us put our energy and focus on what we have and what we enjoy together. Where we don't meet our partner's needs, let them find their way and meet them. He brings his excitement back to our relationship. I never say to Jim he can't do something. I think if I denied him, it wouldn't be a good thing. I can dialogue about it, but I can't say 'No'. It may be something very important to him. I don't feel hurt by it because he's not being any different with me.

Jim

There's a guy with whom I'm getting very connected. It doesn't feel as romantic as it feels like a 'heart expansion.' We've spent two weekends together. It doesn't feel that de-stabilizing, but Wayne and I talk about it and what it means to our relationship. Wayne doesn't put constraints on me, but I put constraints on myself. Wayne is okay as long as the outside involvement doesn't threaten our relationship.

PARTICIPANTS' DEGREE OF INVOLVEMENT

75% - study couples had rules or norms that precluded or limited involvement
18% - study couples had no restrictions on involvement
7% - had never discussed the issue of emotional involvement

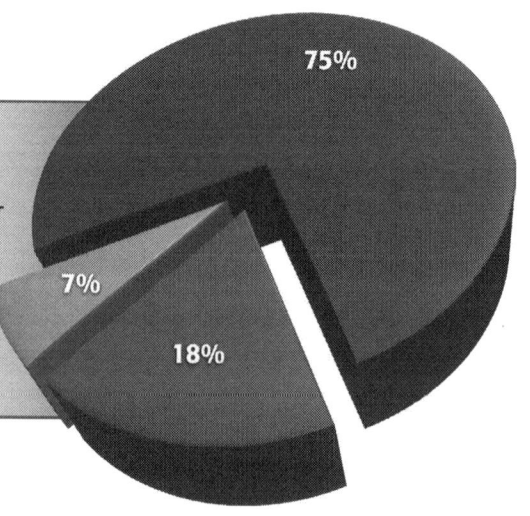

Getting involved as a couple

Some couples found themselves getting involved with a third – as a couple. When couples are getting connected to the same person at the same time, it may feel less threatening to the relationship. We were surprised at the number of couples (13%) who reported having 'a boy' or taking on a third for a period of time. Some of these couples clearly had restrictions against involvement, but their norm was over-ridden by their shared interest and enjoyment. Several couples stated this was an anomaly and didn't expect it to happen again. Some couples had a number of 'boys' over the years.

> We don't fall in love with anyone else, but we've had instances where we've become emotionally attached, but we've always done it together. For awhile we had a third living with us.

> We found a guy we care about and love. He's more than a trick. He's a dear friend. We both love him, but we're not in love with him. We certainly don't love him like we do each other; he's more like our boy – he's 32 and naïve. We watch out for him – have him over for dinner or to play. He is the only one we feel that way about. We'd love to see him find a relationship of his own.

> Emotional involvement is the last thing either of us would want. The only exception was with a neighbor we had 6 years into the relationship. We both liked him very much. We had many 3-somes together and he would spend weekends with us. We tried to keep him connected to both of us equally, but in the second year he became more emotionally involved with me. We ended the relationship at that point because it was hurtful to John. It was the best thing to do. We're still friends, but the sex stopped as soon as he developed romantic feelings toward me.

> We met a guy in '96 that we started to see a lot for 3 months. He was new to the area. He spent every weekend with us, until we felt he was starting to get emotionally involved. We weren't looking for a 3-way relationship and so we had to pull back. We didn't see him for a couple of months, but after that we all became friends again. Eventually, he met someone else and we've maintained our relationship with him. He was the best man at our wedding and our commitment ceremony.

Triads and polyamorous families

A small, but significant number of study couples had enlarged their relationship to include and embrace new members. They felt like they could love and 'be in love' with more than one person (some couples labeled this polyamorous). A third or possibly more people were incorporated into the 'family'. For some this was situational, "we both fell in love with him". For others, it was intentional.

Although one might assume these were couples where 'anything goes', in fact, these 'families' took considerable time to communicate, problem-solve, and build trust and commitment.

> We had a rule that there wouldn't be any emotional involvement. I used to worry that Dale would get attached if he had a really good outside experience. When we met Adrian, we both agreed that he was different. The three of us have been together for 4 years and I expect to be with the two of them the rest of my life. We're monogamous at this point (no longer have 'outside sex'). The three of us all go to therapy, individually and together as needed.

Although we only interviewed a small number of couples or families that fit this model, we talked with 2-3 times that many about participating. The model deserves its own study since the philosophy, dynamics, and issues are quite different from many of our study couples.

Joe

Thom and I were together for 5 years before we met Trent. Trent has been with us for the last 8 years. He's a senior exec at a Fortune 500 company and routinely takes us both to the company's retreats. He introduces us as his 'two husbands'. Sometimes we all do things together and sometimes it's just two of us (any two of us). Our families have been very supportive. They saw how loyal and caring Trent and Thom were when I had cancer.

Thom

I have two husbands. A stool with 3 legs is stronger. We all balance each other. I'm playful even though I have a backbone of steel. Joe and Trent are the adults. Trent is in Denver four days a week, but when we're together with Trent, we're really together. We still have outside sex and various connections, but the three of us are emotionally monogamous.

Trent

It's been a hard year with Joe's health problems. Thom and I alternated 12 hour shifts when Joe was in the hospital and he needed a lot of support when he came home. I don't know how we would have done it if there weren't three of us. It's definitely made us all stronger.

Carl

Walt is my husband, but I have two other major relationships – Chase is my 'boy'. I'm in love with him. Chase is in a 10-year relationship with my best friend. I'm also in love with Nelson, my other boy. We all view ourselves as family. Walt and I don't keep anything from each other. The 5 of us are very, very close. There are a variety of relationships, not all sexual, but all intimate.

Walt

When Carl tells me about someone new, I can't help thinking "Oh dear God, are you falling in love with another one?"' That's when Carl usually says, "I'm going to slap you if you roll your eyes again." No, I'm not threatened by it. Carl is incredibly loyal and I know we're in it for the long haul.

Leonard

I was with my ex-partner Taylor, when I met Phillip. I've always considered myself polyamorous and so for the first four years that Phillip and I were together, I was still with Taylor. The three of us got along well together. Our relationship is definitely wide open, but it's not anything goes as in 'whatever'. We're very responsible and committed to what we have. The norms we have:

- Honesty. A very proactive honesty that includes consistent checking in.

- Trying to integrate, rather than compartmentalize. If I have a relationship that is becoming serious, I need to introduce that person to the family and they need to welcome them in (or not). If they're not comfortable with the person than it won't work.

- Consideration and respect. Each of us is good about sharing time with the others. They have their own relationships with each other (non-sexual), and are respectful of each one's relationship with me.

Anything is fine if it adds to what we have here. If I (or someone else) was to get involved with someone in a way that jeopardized what we have, we wouldn't do it.

Phillip

We consciously defined ourselves as open from the beginning. Each of us is free to see others within the boundary of not upsetting the whole. My previous partners were into the drama of jealousy, which just doesn't work for me. Leonard was with Taylor when we met. The three of us became a triad. It worked really well and I was really sad when Taylor decided not to continue.

Approaches to Rules & Norms

Explicit rules are one way couples can manage expectations, behaviors, and fears. In what little research that has been done on non-monogamy, rules and explicit agreements have been a central focus. However, we found less reliance on explicit rules than what the research assumes.

> **APPROACHES TO RULES AND NORMS**
> 32% - had explicit rules
> 43% - had norms or understandings
> 15% - had very fluid, emergent rules
> 10% - eschewed rules

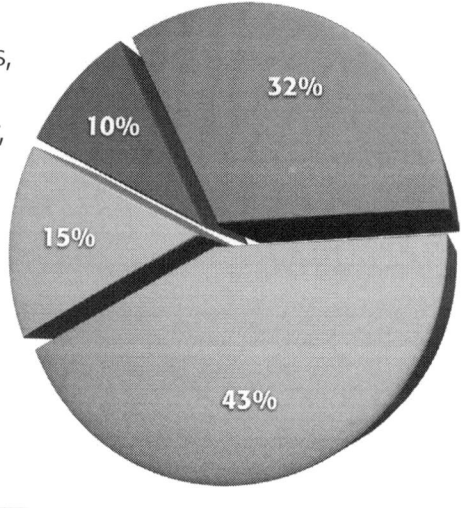

No rules

In fact, 10% of our study couples were explicitly disdainful of rules:

> I wouldn't be comfortable with a bunch of rules. You'd be constantly watching out for the rules and whose breaking them and then you would have to punish them. Who wants to focus on any of that?

> I hate all those rules! Who cares? Either the relationship is open or it's not.

> We have no rules. If we did, it would put restrictions on each other and we don't want to do that. I want to support Clay in whatever he wants to do. Even if Clay were to meet someone else, I would want the best for him and would support him.

Emergent rules

15% of couples had fluid, emergent rules. In general, they hadn't talked through norms and had no set guidelines. This left them with a general fuzziness about what exactly might be okay, but within the context of "we're pretty relaxed about all this". For example, what to disclose after going out might be ambiguous. "Sometimes I share and sometimes I don't - it depends on the situation."

Although things are left rather loose, a rule might emerge in response to a particular situation or problem. An example might be requiring a partner to stop seeing someone with whom he was getting too involved.

> For the first couple of years there was an assumption of monogamy – at least I had an assumption we would be monogamous. What was clear is that we would be completely honest with each other and we did that. There were occasional 'outside sex' exceptions and then we would talk about it. It was difficult and some of it was painful. I often got very emotional. I especially got angry when I found out Thierry had sex with a former boyfriend. Rationally, I thought it was okay, but emotionally, it hurt. After a number of these experiences, we came to our first rule: "To talk about it ahead of time".

Spoken & unspoken norms

43% of couples had at least a few norms – patterned behavior that provided a framework from which to operate. Although they may never have explicitly agreed on a specific rule, they described shared understandings and jointly held values that strongly influenced their thinking and behavior.

> We don't really have defined rules. We do have the norm of playing together. We played apart some early on, but we realized we'd rather keep it inside. We shifted to playing together about a year into the relationship. We want to keep our sex drive in the relationship. It's not a rule, but I think we have a shared understanding about playing together and what's priority.

> There are no rules or restrictions around emotional involvement, but there is concern. We both love each other and we know since we're not having sex with each other, there is a potential to fall in love. I did meet someone I fell in love with. I certainly wasn't going to pack up, but I got very emotionally involved. I've learned to pay attention.

> Our basic policy is to try and play together. It's okay if something presents itself when you're on your own, but we don't put much energy there. It has to be respectful. It's not okay to suck everything in sight and it's not okay to leave the other person sitting at home while you go cruise. It's not really rules-based, but we have a pretty good understanding.

> We don't have set rules around it, but we choose not to have affairs. You can see the flags go up when someone is getting emotionally involved, and we pull ourselves back. The agreement is: be careful; don't get too involved and jeopardize the relationship.

> We don't really have rules, but we both realize that we're dedicated to each other. It's been an understanding that's developed. If something happens (individual sex), eventually, we will talk about it. At first it was kind of scary, but then we got over it. It's just sex. The first fear was one of us would get emotionally attached, but now we realize our emotional attachment is to each other only. We have fuck buddies, but we don't see them outside of a sexual context. They don't become social friends. For us, that would signify an emotional attachment.

Clear rules

32% of couples had rules and found them helpful for guiding behavior, reassuring one another and building a greater foundation of trust.

We set down some rules when we first agreed:
- If we go out together; we come home together
- If we go out together and one wants to go off or stay out longer, we want to know where he is going and what to expect.
- We enjoy each other, but if something comes along – we take advantage.
- We only do 3-ways if we both agree on the person.
- We talk about if it we've done something – always above board
- If one of us is on holiday, it's okay to have outside sex (partner is back home).

We have the same norms we began with. Nothing has changed
- No anal intercourse with outsiders (it's our way of protecting ourselves from a health perspective)
- Only go out when one is traveling or out of town
- If we're together, we play together. Although we do go to the sauna together, and sometimes play separately while we're both there.
- Not allowed to see someone more than once.
- If you arrange to meet that same person again, that's not okay – that's an affair. No planning.

Our spoken rules: When we go out together, we come home together. We tend to stick pretty close to each other. Whether at the baths or a party, we can go off for a little while, but then check back. We touch base a lot.

Our unspoken rules: When we travel, it's okay to fool around (either of us). We don't need to tell or inform the other unless it's extremely hot, tragic, or silly.

Setting the rules ahead of time in terms of what we would and would not do was very important. For example, neither of us will get fucked. We feel that part of our relationship is a 'sacred thing' that we only want to do with each other.

The rules change

Although some couples stay consistent with their initial rules, many find the rules evolve as they discover first-hand what works, doesn't work, and what's actually needed:

Sean

We originally started with a bunch of rules. No one can spend the night. Nobody more than twice. That lasted about a year and then one day I came home and Chuck asked me about a guy he met online. It was my ex-boyfriend. We invited him for the weekend and had a great time. He still comes and stays with us a couple times a year and is a good friend. It's okay to play separately, but we put most of our energy into three-ways. We have a number of friendships that are sexual with the two of us, but not separately. We only play without the other when it just happens at the gym or traveling. We don't develop friendships without the other.

Chuck

Our initial rules evolved. Now we don't always play together, but most of the time. It's okay to do someone multiple times. We have friends with benefits and we've often had guys come and visit and stay with us for the weekend. The rule around that is they sleep in the guest room. Things are pretty fluid. If we're both attracted to someone, than that person has to want to play with both of us.

Stewart

We have pretty clear rules, although they're evolving:

- Twice is the limit to see any particular person, although Lee found guys he liked playing with that I met and didn't feel were a threat and so we began allowing fuckbuddies.
- The overnight rule has evolved to its okay when you're out of town.
- The anal sex rule has remained, but I would very much like to change it. Lee's not into anal sex, but I'm getting increasingly into it. It's getting harder for me not to do it. Tricks will say, "But no one will ever know." But of course, I would know. We talk about it periodically.

Lee

- We always tell each other, including the details.
- I always tell whoever I am playing with that I am partnered and I will be telling him.
- We have to play safe. This means no marks, which is a big concession for me.
- Emotional connection is strong because of S/M. The two-time rule saves me. The two-time rule doesn't apply when traveling and it also includes grey for fuck buddies. I have several buddies that I've become friends with. Stewart has met them and isn't threatened by them and they have been integrated into our lives. Stewart doesn't mind if I play with them more than once.

Or fall away

Some couples who start with rules evolve to a place where they are comfortable without them. Over time, they develop a good idea of what to expect, a deeper trust in their partner, and a confidence that they will be able to address issues on a case-by-case basis. The rules may no longer be necessary because both partners are following the spirit behind the rules.

> At first, Jack hardly played out at all, but he did make a bunch of rules for me to play by. But over the years, we relaxed them all. The only rule left is that there be no overnight stays. However, it's okay to spend the night at a trick's, if the other person is out of town. Ironically, now, Jack is the only one going out.

> There are no rules now. But we act based on our feelings for each other. We act respectfully – appreciate each other's needs. We won't do things we know might be hurtful, e.g. dating someone or getting emotionally involved. I want him to be happy and do whatever he needs to be happy.

Typical Rules & Norms

Each couple has to develop and customize their own approach to non-monogamy. Norms were often where couples were the most creative. Injunctions are typically serious and impersonal but given we're gay men, negotiated agreements often had a playful edge or matter-of-fact bluntness. Before sharing the most typical rules, we'd like to share some of the less common rules that joyfully reflect our gay sensibilities.

Ms. Manners' Top Ten List

10. You can see him as many times as you want, but you can't schedule it
9. If they're in our bed when I get home, they're fair game
8. If you're in love with the guy, you're not allowed to fuck with him one-on-one
7. You can put him in the sling, but no cuddling
6. If you bring him home and he's cute, you have to let me join
5. You can fuck whoever you want, but you can't take him to dinner
4. If you're in the mood to fuck someone else, but I'm horny, you have to do me first
3. You have to spend twice as much time with me than with any of your tricks
2. You're only allowed to date the terminally ill
1. "The Sauna Clause": Sex at the gym doesn't count as sex

Honesty

There were a few very prevalent norms. One was the limiting of emotional involvement, which we discussed previously. Even more prevalent was the norm of Honesty – being straightforward with the truth. Whether or not it was explicitly stated, it was apparent in couples' responses and stories. Often it was mentioned as something that didn't exist in a previous relationship. Even couples that preferred not to share much information, usually had a norm of having to respond truthfully and sufficiently to a partner's questions. Honesty was viewed as foundational.

> Straight away, I just wanted honesty and I never had it before. Dean's always been honest. Sometimes I don't like what he has to tell me, but he always tells me. I had a boyfriend for 18 years who lied and cheated. He was gorgeous and men were all over him and he would pretend nothing was happening.

> We meet people when we're out at parties so another rule is you have to introduce them to me before you leave. That way they clearly know Van has a partner, he has a face and they recognize they are getting permission. This has been valuable because it actually bothers some guys and those are the ones that need to fully recognize that we are partnered. It also gives a clear message that we are being straightforward and that we have agreed upon rules.

Courtesy and consideration

54% of couples with norms mentioned courtesy and consideration. Some couples instinctively practiced this; some had rules that reinforced it.

We're also very considerate. We can be out and if one of us meets someone and the other isn't interested or doesn't find them attractive, it's fine to go home with them. But if we were to meet someone that we both found very attractive, it would be rude for one of us to leave with that person. We make sure that neither of us is going to be hurt.

Courtesy and respect are important. We plan outside sex for times when we're not together. Whatever we want to do together is first priority. If I've played with someone, they need to be courteous to Richard. One guy told Richard he was going to take me away from him and Richard certainly didn't have to tell me not to see him again.

Although we don't have rules, we do have a norm around loyalty. When we're out together, we won't ever leave with someone else or give up any evening to be with a trick, when we could be together. It's partly courtesy, but neither of us would want to do anything that would hurt the other's feelings.

Jose had to learn how to be honest with me and how to remember to keep me in consideration when he did things. There are some unspoken norms now. You have to take me into account. You have to be considerate of my feelings and how it will impact me.

We give each other first choice of time – the right of refusal for any reason. We prefer to spend time together. The right of first refusal? If you're in the mood to fuck someone else, but I'm horny, do it with me first.

We generally try to be courteous and that can be difficult logistically. If I make arrangements to meet someone and then Dallas doesn't have plans and he doesn't have anything to do, I will usually cancel. I would feel guilty. We don't just take off to go have outside sex when we're spending the afternoon together. We try to keep it out of each other's face.

3-way etiquette

Courtesy and consideration were even more carefully cultivated when couples played together with outsiders. Couples had various rules or understandings that ensured each partner felt valued, comfortable and respected.

> We both have to feel comfortable. Either one can call the night. We always check. If Ted stops, I can continue, providing he's comfortable. I never want to have sex if it might make Ted uncomfortable or would hurt him in any way. I value Ted and our relationship much more than the pleasures of sex. If Ted isn't turned on to the guy, but I am and I'm getting revved up, I have to throttle down, which is uncomfortable, but I have no problem calling it off and walking away.

> We're both there whenever we have outside sex and no one does anyone or anything they don't want to do. We attend events together. If one wants to leave, then we would both leave. If something is happening and I can't get past it, then I would or could say, "Let's stop." But usually we enjoy watching each other. We're both insecure individually, but together we're confident.

> Be aware of the other person's feelings, especially if a 3-way. If the differences (older/younger; thinner/stockier) get in the way then it's just not going to work. We just do without, rather than have a conflict.

> We go out as a team. It seems natural that some people will like one of us; some will like the other. We are very comfortable with watching the other play. Sometimes I will handcuff Jim to a chair and watch others play with him. I love to see him 'go for it.'

> Sometimes a person is more attracted to one of us than the other. There are times when Raul really enjoys watching, but we keep track of the other. He will give me a hard pinch and look toward the door if he wants to quit.

Safe sex

43% of couples had rules about safe sex. Some used condoms, some sero-sorted, and some restricted specific behaviors.

Not surprisingly, couples that were HIV negative were more likely to have rules, restrictions, and stronger concerns related to HIV. Of the couples restricting behavior, receptive anal sex was most commonly off limits. A smaller number avoided anal sex altogether and two couples disallowed giving blow jobs.

> We're both negative and want to stay that way. I'm not going to take the risk or break the rule EVER. I've been very cautious since I came out because HIV was already an issue. Health and emotions – we're saving ourselves for each other.

> Sean's concerns are all around health and HIV. We're both HIV negative, but we don't have the same intellectual agreement about HIV transmission, which is the basis for all our rules.

We asked the study participants that had anal sex, about the frequency with which they used condoms.

Predictably, couples that were sero-discordant were more likely to use condoms with each other. Couples where partners were both positive or both negative typically did not use condoms.

STUDY COUPLES'S HIV STATUS
24% - both HIV positive
49% - both HIV negative
27% - mixed antibody status

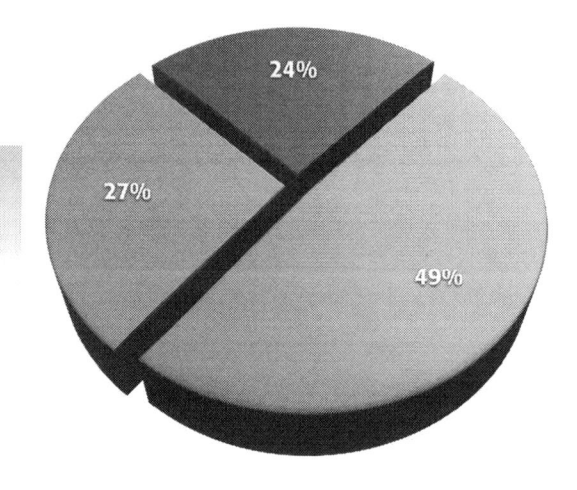

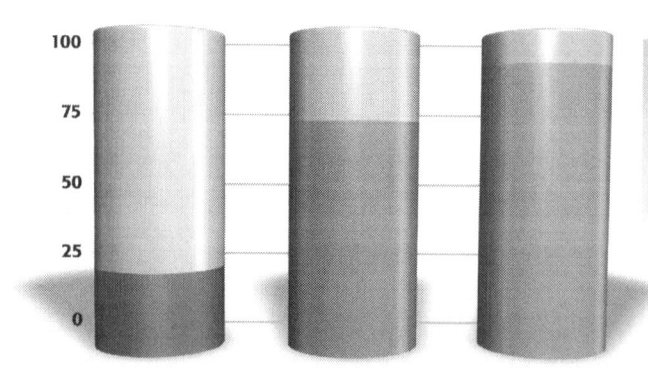

PARTICIPANTS' SAFE SEX PRACTICES
25.3% - frequency participants used condoms **with partner**
71.8% - frequency participants used condoms **with outsider of similar status**
89.7% - frequency participants used condoms **with outsider of opposite status**

Other commonly mentioned norms

Below is a list of other commonly mentioned norms. All are attempts to either:

- limit connection or emotional involvement
- prevent discomfort, hurt feelings, and jealousy; or
- ensure partners practice safe sex

> **Other Commonly Mentioned Norms**
> 32% - Can't bring them home
> 22% - Can't stay out all night
> 20% - Veto rights – We stop if I'm uncomfortable
> 16% - Can't go home with them
> 11% - Can't see them more than once (or twice)
> 11% - Restrictions on specific sex acts, e.g. "No receptive anal sex"
> 11% - Okay to play when out of town

A norm we recommend

We conclude this segment with one norm that we heard from several couples that made good sense to us:

> If things aren't going well between us, it's not a good time to play outside the relationship. I've put off guys, when John and I are having trouble.

> There have been a few times when we were going through rough times in the relationship and we made a point not to go out during those times.

> Primary commitment has always been clear and is even clearer now. Bottom line is: "What's my core commitment?" If we were ever in a place where that was in question or we were having trouble as a couple, that would be a time not to go out. If we were having problems, we shouldn't being going outside, we should be home tending the relationship.

Challenges and Difficulties

We asked participants what they felt was difficult or most challenging about non-monogamy. The top response was Jealousy.

What Is Most Difficult?

21%	Jealousy
20%	One or both getting too emotionally involved
12%	Becoming comfortable with Non-Monogamy
11%	Challenges that arise in 3-ways
9%	Dishonesty
8%	Issues related to Drug/Alcohol Use
7%	Lack of sensitivity
20%	"Nothing has been difficult"

Jealousy

21% of participants said jealousy was a difficulty or had been a difficulty at some point. Based on the research and articles about non-monogamy, we would have expected this number to be higher. Furthermore, many of the participants who mentioned jealousy talked about it as something they had gotten past. However, for some, particularly partners who were competitive, jealousy definitely was a source of tension.

> I can be extremely jealous. Jay tells me what he's done right away, but I have a hard time listening to it. Sometimes I say, "That's enough. I don't want to hear any details." I get really competitive with guys I know that have done him. I compare myself to them and wonder if they're better sex than me. Interestingly, I don't get jealous when we do three-ways. I love to see him having a good time. I love to see two guys having at him and sometimes I may just watch, although usually not. When I see him enjoying himself and having so much fun, I know that's what I want. I guess it over-rides any competitive feelings – I just don't go there.

> Initially it would bother me to see Brent kissing another man. We talked about it and he quickly agreed not to. But over time it became okay with me.

> Occasionally I get jealous when I'm not included. I tell Barrett when it happens and he's good about hearing me and reassuring me.

> He attracts tricks better than me. He's younger. Sometimes feelings of jealousy come up. I have a pang of jealousy when he's been with someone hotter than me and I know he's been getting fucked by someone that he's hot for. But I don't like to hang onto negative emotions. I don't like to let them spiral out of control. I figure it out on my own and drown the feeling with the reminder of how great our relationship is.

Jack

At one point, I set Miles up with a trick I knew he was really hot for. When Miles came back, he went on and on about how wonderful the guy was and I got really jealous. We've learned to share what happened without the enthusiasm, out of respect for the other partner. We both can get jealous and feel insecure at times. It also happens if someone pays attention to one of us more than the other. Not feeling equal is a big trigger. And it was hard sometimes to see Miles getting fucked by someone when it seemed like he was enjoying it more than he did with me.

Miles

Jealousy has been the hardest issue. If one of us had 'too good' of a time or 'gushed' about it, then the other one would get jealous and feel inadequate or insecure. When jealousy comes up, we just talk through it. We don't fight about anything else, so we try to listen to each other and work it out or take it to therapy.

Jealousy - Fear of losing partner

Jealousy is often triggered by the fear of losing out to a rival. 14% mentioned fear of losing their partner to someone else as something they had felt at some point.

> I used to get insecure and worry that Ross would find someone else more attractive and leave me. It's not really an issue now. At the Baths, I love to see Ross get sucked off in the steam room - it doesn't make me jealous at all.

> Jealousy has been hard. I'm the one that gets jealous – it's usually if I see him with someone I think is cute. It's not a competitive jealousy. It's more that I begin to worry where I stand with David. At this point, I realize it isn't likely (to lose David) and I reassure myself. If it really bothers me, I bring it up. David is reassuring. He reminds me it's just sex – it's nothing to do with emotional ties. It's a lot less now. I'd say it was a 10 and now it's a 3.

> I was more interested in other guys than Lewis was and he had this fear that I was going to leave him. Ironically, I think being able to include others took care of my needs such that Lewis is less concerned about me leaving now.

Kurt

> The frequency has been hard. Paul goes to the baths 2-3 times a month. That seems like a lot to me. I really don't understand Paul's interest in the baths and outside sex. Paul has reassured me that he has no intention of falling in love and replacing me. I still need to hear that he won't find 'the new Mr. Right.'

Paul

> The most difficult thing was physically leaving to go to the baths for the first time, knowing that Kurt was at home and unhappy about it. I knew I had to do it in order to be happy but I had to convince Kurt that it wasn't about him. No one could be everything I want.

Jealousy - Envy

Whereas jealousy is about something one has and is afraid of losing, envy refers to wanting what the other one has (or preventing them from having it). 6% of participants mentioned envy or experiences of envy.

> He's hooking up with more guys than me. I'm not jealous. I'm just envious that he's getting it and I'm not. I realize with time, it balances out, but it's my own insecurity.

> At times I would feel envious - he's getting it; he's attractive; he's alive and I'm not.

Jealousy - Insecurity

Jealousy, fear, and envy (and sometimes anger) can get jumbled together. Often the underlying emotion is hurt (My self-worth or position has been injured) or insecurity (I have doubts about my position or self-worth). The emotional reaction may be triggered by the other person's actions, but is rooted in one's own sense of security and self-esteem.

> Feeling insecure was hard. It helped me appreciate my first partner's insecurity.

> Dealing with insecurity. It's more my issue. People are attracted to Rick because he's older, bigger and has a big dick. It's important to remember that Rick loves me enough that he wouldn't leave me.

> Feeling left out and feeling fearful and jealous. It's only been intermittent, but there were definitely times.

> Because I'm older, sometimes when we go out together, people will look at him before they look at me (he's younger and he's better looking than me). So at the sauna, I just let him go do whoever. It doesn't bother me. He's younger and more buff.

> Pat gets jealous. He doesn't understand why I don't. I tell him it's because I trust him. I only want Pat here if he wants to be here. I tell him if he stops loving me, he should move on. I'm secure about who I am and I feel secure in the relationship. I was really sick in the hospital and almost died and Pat was there for me. I know he really loves me.

> For Jack, "It's just sex." He says it's meaningless, but I feel hurt and insecure when he goes out. It really affects my self-esteem. I don't think relationships have to be monogamous, but I do think sex is an important aspect of the relationship and I don't take it lightly.

Dale

> Sometimes it's still hard. I can feel hurt, angry, jealous, envious. It was hard for Chuck because he knew I would have this big emotional reaction and he knows I could be happy being monogamous. I try to understand my reactions and look at how much of it is about self-esteem. I focus on things that make me feel good about myself like my job, my art. It's more to do with how I'm feeling about myself than who or what Chuck does. It's definitely easier if I've been playing around myself. Sometimes I do that prophylactic ally - preventive medicine.

Chuck

> The hardest thing for me is knowing that it sometimes hurts Dale when I go out. We changed our 'honesty rule' to 'we only have to tell when asked'. That's been helpful. I think it's hardest for Dale when I go out when he isn't feeling particularly good about himself. But I still go out.

Jealousy - Antidotes

Interestingly, many brought jealousy up as something they had learned to conquer or keep at bay. Feeling secure seemed to be an antidote. To get there, participants talked about reassurance, building self-esteem, focusing on what they have, and/or feeling generous toward their partner.

Sometimes when they were very attractive, I would be thinking 'Is he a threat to me?' Knowing the fact that he was coming home with me – I reassured myself

It took a lot of self-acceptance and letting go of my insecurities. When I accepted Ron, then I had to look at myself – all the reasons I felt I wasn't good enough, not cute enough, don't have enough hair, not good enough at sex, too heavy. And I came to terms with who I am and where I found value in myself. This has been really important for me.

It helps me to understand my own feelings, where they come from, and how they affect me - but not allow my feelings to take over and control my life. I can recognize I'm feeling angry or jealous, but then I think, "Okay. Enough of this shit. Get over it". I value my relationship and I focus there.

When I get jealous, we back off from going out for awhile until we're both ready to do it again. I remember that at a very deep level I know we're not going to break up, and I also remind myself it's not that big of an issue.

I worry about STDs, but I don't get jealous.. I like that I don't feel the need to 'own' Steven. I believe that you have to want to be together and that people will only stick around if they want to. I don't believe in 'trapping' each other. I don't compete with the guys Steven has sex with – I am who I am and I'm comfortable with that.

Ed was very different from my first love – we're much more honest and grown-up. Sometimes I had trouble knowing what I felt or expressing what I felt. It could be me getting close to someone or Ed getting too close to someone and me feeling hurt. It took a few years to feel more secure. We're quite secure in who we are now. Why? Therapy and practice - realizing it was a different relationship; realizing what I was feeling; remembering I could express it.

My first lover taught me how not to be jealous. We lived in the Castro and he didn't work at an office and he had a notoriously big dick and he was very clear that he wanted an open relationship. I loved this man so much I decided I couldn't deny this love because of jealousy. I discovered I could have a relationship and have a lot of sex with a lot of other people."

I occasionally get jealous around Jerry and I've learned to take that as a signal I need more time with him or reassurance. Jealousy is a very transitory emotion if you don't feed into it.

I feel secure in the relationship. If someone could make him happier through sex & take him away, then we didn't have much going on in the first place."

I just ignore my jealousy. I deal with it and go to sleep and the next day it's gone.

Discomfort with non-monogamy

12% of participants described difficulties becoming comfortable with non-monogamy or the decision to open the relationship. Some participants described initial discussions as what was most difficult. Some spoke of internal conflicts about being non-monogamous. Some reported that openly sharing information and expressing feelings was difficult. And a few reported that their differences about opening the relationship were still unresolved.

Just getting clear at the beginning. It's gotten increasingly comfortable. I don't feel any jealousy.

Talking about it, especially at the beginning. Coming up with the ground rules was hard.

At first, it's getting over the idea of having an open relationship. In my previous relationships, we were never open. However, I got over this. The first couple of times we played alone at a sauna it was a little uncomfortable, but it was easier since we were both in the same location. Otherwise, it's never really caused an issue for us.

There's still a part of me that feels like I'm doing something wrong. I can come home feeling sleazy. It's not about the couple, but a little voice saying "There's no commitment; It's just casual; Is this good for us?"

Being open and communicating and sharing feelings is hard for me. Sometimes I can do it and sometimes Ryan has to guess what I'm feeling and draw it out of me.

Coming to a level of acceptance. I was raised in a charismatic Christian church. Being gay and sex outside of marriage were both wrong. I've had to realize that's not the case for everyone. It's taken work. I had to change my morals, e.g. I had to decide it's okay not to be restricted to one person.

What's still difficult is Ray sometimes gets emotionally upset because I'm going out. He wished I wouldn't or that I would do it less often. He feels hurt by it. On the other hand, he's not all that interested in sex with me when I initiate it. We've had an agreement to be open for 25 years, but it's not resolved. I try to compromise or negotiate. Sometimes he gets upset and sometimes it doesn't bother him.

It feels like being open is a threat to our relationship – it's definitely a source of tension. Right now I feel guilty because he's not going out much so does that mean he's more invested in the relationship than I am? It's a question of weighing the needs of each individual with the needs of the relationship.

Connor

I spend an undue amount of time thinking about it and worrying about it. I spend lots of time on the computer trying to hook up and planning it so it won't be in Logan's face. Logan thought we needed to break up. We went to a counselor for 5 sessions and worked through some of the issues.

We eventually agreed to have an open relationship. However, we are still working out the rules.

Logan

I recognize and remember the good things we have. It's way too much to throw out. I chose not to leave the relationship even though Connor is strongly committed to continuing to go out. Of course, it would have been better if we had firm agreements on the front-end.

The challenges of 3-ways

11% of participants reported difficulties when playing as a couple with outsiders. Finding the outsider can be challenging and how the outsider relates to both partners can trigger many of the same feelings of jealousy and insecurity mentioned previously. Some couples avoid playing together for this reason; others become skilled at paying close attention to these dynamics.

> We soon realized that we needed to play separately. Being a mixed race couple made it difficult to do three-ways. People weren't attracted to me or sometimes they would only be attracted to me. Stan is more outgoing and people find that attractive. He would bring them in, but often they would only be interested in him. I was treated poorly. I had to come to terms with it and realize it was their problem – but it meant playing separately. Stan didn't realize the disconnect because he was into the moment of relating to them. It wasn't that he was insensitive, but he was oblivious and I had to make him aware. On rare opportunities we find someone who is attracted to both of us and we can play together. It's a real treat. There's more of a connectedness with that person and we can share the experience together.

> Learning to make sure everyone is involved. Once in Amsterdam, we were doing a 3-way and I noticed Wayne stepped outside. I went outside and he explained that he felt left out and it was okay for me to continue. I told him we started together and we will finish together and brought him back in. I reassured him and I've learned to pay attention to how involved everyone feels.

> We have such different types that it was really difficult when we only played together. We've also had issues when the third liked one of us more than the other. They don't need to like us both equally, but they have to be respectful and join with both of us.

> It's hard to find guys we're both sexually compatible with. A lot of guys don't like 3-ways and it might be easier to just play independently. We've discussed it, but we don't want to dissipate our sexual energy elsewhere. We're still sexual together and like to spend a lot of time together.

Dishonesty

9% of participants mentioned a point in their relationship when they, their partner, or the two of them were not being fully forthright about their outside sex. Examples included covert outside sex prior to opening the relationship (discussed previously), illicit affairs (most of which eventually surfaced), not abiding to agreed upon rules, and partners used to habitual outside sex having trouble fully disclosing.

> Initially, I played around and then lied about it. It really takes a long time to regain the trust of your partner after you've lied.

> Les not being honest with me early on was very difficult. As trust with each other grows, we understand each other better, although it's been hard.

> After we opened it up, Skip began to break the rules – on numerous occasions. We still have rules, although I'm not sure Skip always follows them.

Drug/Alcohol issues

8% of respondents mentioned difficulties with drug use related to outside sex. In most cases, crystal (methamphetamine) cocaine and alcohol were the drugs that were problematic. Most of the participants that brought this up were at least several years into abstinence and/or recovery. They reported heavy drug use in previous periods of their lives, difficulties with others who were heavy users, and/or the prevalence of unsafe sex when high. A few participants acknowledged current drug use and their on-going need to curtail or manage this when being sexual.

> Early on, it was insecurity around the relationship. If its once every few months – no problem, but there was a period when Taylor was doing crystal meth and having a lot of outside sex. It was a big deal. I finally told him it was rehab or the end of the relationship. He went into a program and has never slipped in the last 6 years.

> We had to end the relationship with the guy when it became apparent that he wouldn't do anything without being high – not even see a movie.

> We were partying and having group sex when we met. We were seriously involved with crystal and crack, but soon after we met, we both stopped using. Now we depend on each other.

> Drugs and alcohol have always been a part of the scene when we played outside. We used condoms about 70% of the time, but the other 30% of the time was terribly unsafe.

> I've been in recovery for 8 years, but it still comes up. Sex and drugs used to be synonymous for me – I couldn't do one without the other. I'm still re-claiming sex from 'sex and drugs'.

Lack of sensitivity

7% mentioned their partner's insensitivity. It wasn't seen as intentional, but more a general lack of awareness – a pattern of being so focused on their own concerns and pleasure, they forget to track or take into account the impact an action might have on their partner. In most cases, although the partner learned to be more aware and less insensitive, it continues as an on-going issue rearing its head periodically.

> I'm pretty aware of Xavier. If anything I do might hurt him, I will stop. I think Xavier is less sensitive. He lives in the moment much more than I do.

> Initially Tom saw everything through his own lens and didn't include me in the equation when he made decisions. He's learning to take my feelings into account.

> When Tim got too involved, I had to let him know it hurt me. He's more emotionally available than me and so it's hard for him to compartmentalize sex. But I'm more self-aware. I can tell when something isn't the right thing to do. I may do it anyway, but it won't even occur to Tim that something isn't the right thing to do.

Other responses

Two other responses to the question about difficulties were common. 20% mentioned one or both partners getting too emotionally involved. We addressed this previously in the section on Connection and Involvement.

For another 20%, the response was: "Nothing. It's never been a problem."

> Nothing has been too hard. I'd say not being explicitly open for all those years was the most difficult thing. I always wanted to be open sooner.

> Outside sex really hasn't been difficult. The biggest issue is trying to spice up our own sex life and keep it active.

> We've never had a big fight about the issue. We may have had disagreements about the timing, but opening the relationship hasn't been a big source of tension.

What Helps

We asked couples what helped make non-monogamy work for them. Many participants gave a comprehensive list of factors. Below are a few representative lists followed by the key themes we heard about What Helps:

- We're easy-going and non emotional about outside sex.
- We communicate a lot, which is key. We realize the benefits to the relationship of communicating.
- We use our outside sexual experiences to fuel our own at-home sex.
- We have a high level of trust in each other, but we don't take each other for granted.

- Having a clear understanding of the arrangement takes away the difficulties.
- We make a clear distinction between emotional and physical needs.
- We constructively talk about the issues when we need to.
- We're both physically driven men (sexually), but we're both solidly committed to the emotional aspects of our relationship. We're on the same page on this.

- Discussing it openly.
- Establishing a firm foundation of trust
- Taking it slowly
- We know we always want to be together
- We recognize and differentiate between sex and love
- We developed clear norms that we could follow

What Helps:

%		%	
65%	Communicating Openly and Honestly	18%	Learning to deal with Jealousy – Building Self-Esteem
65%	Being Truthful/Honest	18%	Getting Support from Therapists or Mentors
52%	Trusting (each other and the relationship)	17%	Setting Ground rules
34%	Reassurance & Appreciation	6%	Practicing Moderation
30%	Respecting Partner and their differences		

Communicating openly and honestly

The most common response was honest, open communication. 65% included this in their response to the question about what helps.

> Communication! Honesty! Openness! The more we talk the better we feel. Knowing there are no surprises or secrets makes it much easier. I would have big problems if I didn't know who or what Elliot was doing outside the relationship.

> Talking about it and being honest. If there's a problem, surface it, rather than gunny sacking it. If you can talk about this, it makes talking about other issues that much easier. It's really important to talk honestly, why you want to have outside sex, what it means to you, and then jointly decide the parameters.

> The ability to communicate effectively. We can get pissy and childish, but then we pull back and work it out. One of our great strengths is we have the ability to talk openly about potentially difficult things without getting dramatic. We hear each other's concerns and sometimes we have to put it aside and come back when we're calmer, but we always come back and resolve it. In previous relationships, those fractures never got healed. We're able to resolve things and move on.

> It's important to me that we've stayed connected and in good communication with each other about outside sex. We have grown together in this area rather than grown separately. This has allowed us to incorporate outside sex in a healthy way.

> We're honest about everything, even if it bothers the other person. We didn't used to communicate well. We would argue about doing the dishes, when that wasn't the real issue.

> After 15 years, there's a lot more understanding: "Oh, it's your back that's hurting; it's not about me." It's painful for me to not talk and it's painful for Allen to talk. So we've had to learn how to talk while trying not to overdo it. We've learned how to communicate. And when I get really pissed, I have to remember how much I love him.

> You have to talk it through. Nothing is off the table - being straightforward and trustful and honest even if your first impulse is fear or shame.

> We learned how to communicate with each other 17 years ago. We were both from highly dysfunctional families, but we learned from our 12-step programs how to communicate. We have a common language.

> Being able to talk things out. I will tell Dean if I feel he's falling in love with someone. If it's serious, Dean will figure it out. And Dean sees my patterns and knows what's going on. He helps me through these situations.

Frequency of relationship discussions

We also asked couples to rate the frequency with which they discussed relationship issues (regardless of topic). Below are participants' responses. A few observations:

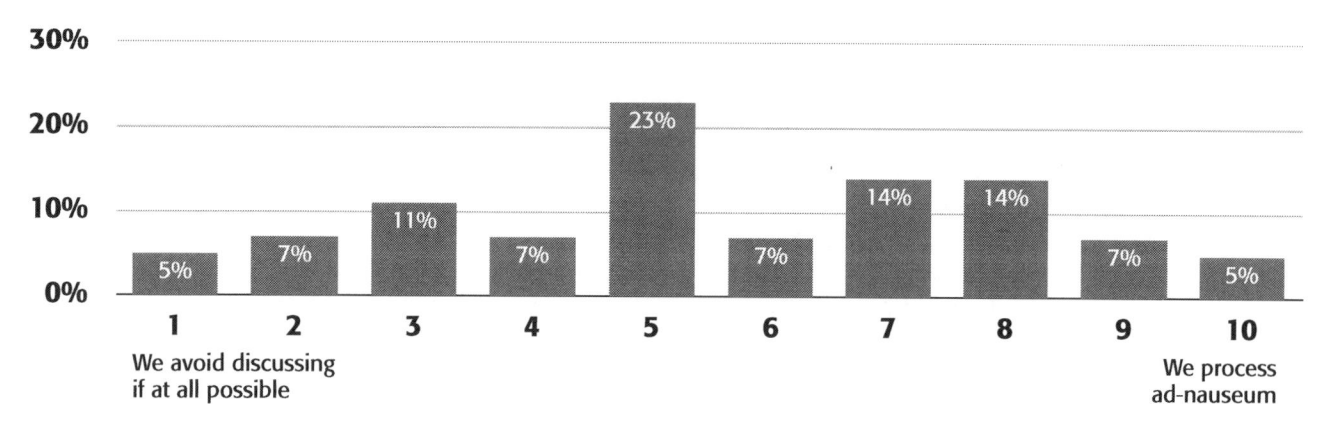

Score	Percentage
1 — We avoid discussing if at all possible	5%
2	7%
3	11%
4	7%
5	23%
6	7%
7	14%
8	14%
9	7%
10 — We process ad-nauseum	5%

- Couples scoring lower often commented "We don't have many issues".
- Couples scoring lower tended be the ones that disclosed less about outside sex.
- Couples scoring higher were more comfortable with difficult conversations, more likely to form connections with outsiders and enjoyed sharing their internal experience
- Most of the '1' scores were only one partner – not both, and often indicated concern – "We don't talk enough."
- Approximately 20% of the couples had strong differences where one partner preferred relationship discussions more than the other. This could be a source of friction, but most commented on how they had found a middle ground.

Being truthful/honest

Honesty was often linked with comments about communication, but it was also mentioned separately, in its own right. 65% spoke about the importance of being truthful.

> Being honest. The more I was honest, the less problems we had.

> We've done a really good job of being honest and being honest about our emotions. You have to be honest to make it work, given our rules. It's the whole continuum from "Who do you find attractive?" to "I'm feeling very emotionally involved and don't want to stop seeing him." Being that honest has helped build trust in the foundation of our relationship.

> We're totally honest and that has really helped. We lay out the 'warts and all' for each other to see.

> Honesty is the most important. Not just saying everything, but understanding the other person's feelings and concerns and sharing things in a considerate manner. Knowing that I will have to tell Walt, keeps me from doing certain things. I know whatever I do, I will have to tell him, so it helps me draw the boundary. It helps me avoid unsafe sex or doing someone he wouldn't approve of in a public place.

> We both had prior relationships where partners cheated. Neither of us wanted that again. We've always been open and honest with each other for that reason.

> The thing that supported us and was bedrock was our agreement about mutual honesty. I knew I would tell him and I knew he would tell me, no matter how uncomfortable it was going to make either of us.

Trust

52% of participants named 'Trust' in response to the question "What helps?" Trust, which is an important ingredient in any relationship seems pivotal in a non-monogamous relationship. Participants talked about trust as both an action and an outcome. An active belief in their partner's love and integrity reassured them when they might be feeling fearful or insecure.

> I trust that Pete wouldn't go out on me. I trust him 100%.

> I trust in the 'concern for the other'. I trust Bill is deeply concerned about my happiness.

> We have an absolute trust in each other and in our relationship. We trust that we can work out any issues that come up.

> You have to build trust in a relationship and ultimately you have to let go. You can't be insecure really or jealous or it won't work. I experienced all that early on, but it's all about building trust. Yes, there's a danger that the relationship could end, but if you want to have the ability to go out, then you have to learn to trust the other person. It takes time and a certain commitment to the relationship.

> There's always going to be something else with this issue. Its trial and error and you have to push the boundaries occasionally and trust that if it becomes a problem we will work it out and self-correct. Trust that it won't jeopardize the on-going relationship and the intention for it to continue.

Trust as an outcome

Trust as an outcome was built through consistent love, caring and commitment. If partners were consistently honest with each other, trust deepened. We heard repeatedly from couples, as their experience of successfully trusting each other grew, it became easier to manage the ambiguity of an open relationship.

> The two times I got too involved, I stopped because Paul told me I had to. That actually increased the trust in the relationship because now he knew I would stop if he asked and I became more aware and committed to paying attention. The depth of our trust wouldn't be possible without having gone through that test. We've learned to respect each other's concerns.

> Opening up the relationship has been a hurdle, but once you work your way through it, you know you can work through anything and the trust factor goes up tenfold.

> Although it was easy to come to agreement, being open from the beginning made it tougher to build the relationship. There wasn't a deep foundation of trust to rely on. We had to get comfortable telling the other person what we had done and we had to get comfortable hearing it. But this allowed the trust to happen and the foundation to develop.

> We were sure we would stay together, so that helped because we didn't worry about that. That probably fell in place after about 10 years of being together.

> It's allowed us to be more trusting of each other. You always know at the end of the day that the other person will be at home there for you. They aren't going anywhere. It's actually made our relationship stronger.

> We're probably more stable because of the struggles around outside sex. It gave us both the opportunity to show the other that we had some restraint. I've had 2 or 3 guys that I was seeing a few times, 'propose' to me. I had to tell them that I must not have made myself completely clear and then ended the connection.

> We feel very attuned. I don't feel we will ever break up. We complement each other. Our connection is so strong. I think all this allows us to trust each other.

Appreciation and reassurance

Appreciation of their partner and the relationship was a key support for 34% of participants. The relationship and life created together was reassuring - helping them look past the smaller issues and keep things in perspective. Sometimes individuals needed to be reminded of their partner's love and loyalty, e.g. "I needed to hear that he wouldn't leave me." But often they reminded and reassured themselves.

> We've seen a lot of our friends break up and then wished they hadn't. It makes us appreciate what we have and so we give each other a little more space because we know we value each other and our relationship. It helps us trust that we're both going to come home.

> We have similar values, a similar sense of integrity. We really appreciate who the other person is.

> Focusing on the big picture of the relationship helps. I can't imagine ever being happy with anyone but Phillip. I've never met anyone else that I would want to spend my life with. It puts the outside sex in perspective. I know why outside sex is important to Phillip, but more importantly is why I'm with Phillip and that has allowed outside sex to be relatively easy to deal with.

It probably doesn't get talked about much, but there is the reassurance of time passing. We're still coming home; we still love each other; we're still going about the day-to-day of living our lives together.

The commitment of not ever leaving allowed us to get rid of fear. At year #5, I told Taylor that "I'm in regardless." From that point on, I was no longer going to ever entertain the notion that bailing was an option. It laid a foundation and the fear of talking about difficulties or being completely honest about anything went away.

We realize our relationship is strong at the foundation. The primary commitment has always been clear and is even clearer now.

We always did a great deal together regardless of any problems in this arena and that was helpful. We had a lot else that was good and that fueled our love and trust and commitment.

Respecting partner and their differences

30% of participants named respect as an important helper. Participants spoke of respecting a partner's feelings and sensibilities, but also acknowledging and honoring a partner's differences.

The key for us is we have respect for each other and for each other's feelings. We've stayed committed and we follow our agreements.

I had to really respect what he wants or doesn't want. He has to take time to process and he doesn't like being surprised. He tends to see things in black and white – he knows something is either right or wrong for him. He won't do something he really doesn't want to do. I was pushing the boundaries and so I had to make sure he was comfortable with the changes. If he's insecure or pissed, I will know it and I need to reassure him.

We both have strong personalities and we've adapted to each other. We had to get to a place where it is okay to disagree and realize that neither of us is wrong, we just have different views.

I've seen other couples where one person becomes too tolerant of their partner. It's vital to speak up; to take a stand; "There are certain things I will not allow. There are certain things that are deal-breakers". Examples? Inattention – being emotionally left out; Not being treated as a partner in all ways; Respect.

Both people have to be willing to accept that they are going to grow and change. The reason our relationship works is because we both want the other to grow and experience their dreams. Tony is very secure and doesn't get jealous. Because he's so trusting, it gives me a lot of latitude to explore myself.

Respecting each other's opinions and styles is critical. We make a habit of communicating preferences in the moment and we consider the other person's feelings a lot. We check in, "Are you okay?" - My partner's opinion matters as much as my own.

Getting support

18% of participants talked about getting outside support. This took two forms. Some utilized therapists and counselors (separately or as a couple). Some had friends or mentors that they felt they could confide in and use as a sounding board. The enthusiasm of couples who had mentors was in marked contrast to the couples who complained of feeling isolated and unable to find couples who would talk openly.

> Being able to talk with other couples about how they handle the issue helps us normalize. Rather than demonize the outside sex, as we were raised, they were supportive. It helped to hear, "It's not about 'infidelity' or 'cheating' which are derogatory terms; it's about 'play'. Couples counseling has also helped.

> We were lucky enough to have mentors. Our friends supported us and talked with us about it. They said, "Our biggest regret was we didn't allow ourselves to explore when we had the most opportunities. We waited until we had overcome our insecurities." We tried to learn from that and not be quite so cautious.

> Having mentors was a big help. We knew them for five years. One passed away, but we still have Tom and his new partner. We used them as a sounding board. We could see where we stood in relation to them.

> We always knew we really loved each other. I knew Graham was the right guy for me. We weren't sure we were going to make it in the first few years. Our friends certainly didn't think so. But we went to couples counseling because we knew we wanted to make it work together.

> Couples counseling allowed us or taught us how to communicate well and that made a huge difference.

> We did a couple of sessions with a therapist I was seeing for school. That was helpful. It gave us a foundation and helped us develop communication tools (listening and hearing each other).

Don't overdo it

6% of participants mentioned practicing moderation. A few couples talked about periods where they had overdone it. A few participants intimated they thought their partner went out too frequently and/or was compulsive around sex. None of the study couples had rules about overall frequency, but many had norms about what seemed appropriate.

> You need to be with other sex partners, but not 'go crazy'. You need to know when to stop and how to control yourself or you'll ruin your relationship. It goes to respecting your partner.

> We use it as a treat when we're out of town. It's a way of having fun, as opposed to being on a constant quest for sex. We see some couples that are constantly on the hunt; they have to have a third in order to have sex with each other.

> I do think that because we're a couple there should be some restraint. Saying 'No' every once in awhile is a way of valuing the relationship. A couple of times, I've brought it up, "Look we have a relationship, at least say 'No' to going out sometimes." Like after he's been away for a weekend and going out and then not going out at home the next weekend, in addition.

> We don't overtly go looking. We enjoy going out with each other and being with each other. If a third person presents themselves and decides they're interested – fine. This is partly about courtesy and partly about keeping the focus on us as couple enjoying the moment.

Other helpers

- Learning to Deal with Jealousy and building self-esteem was mentioned by 18% of participants. (See section on jealousy for examples and discussion).

- Setting Ground rules was mentioned by 17%. (See sections on Approaches to Rules/Norms and Typical Rules for discussion and examples).

Couples' Sex Lives Together

What about couples own sex lives together?

To get a sense of how outside sex fit in with study couples' own sex lives together, we asked each participant to tell us what percent of their sex was with their partner, independent of their partner, with their partner and others.

- For some, independent sex is primary.
- Some have no, or very little independent sex.
- For others it falls somewhere in between

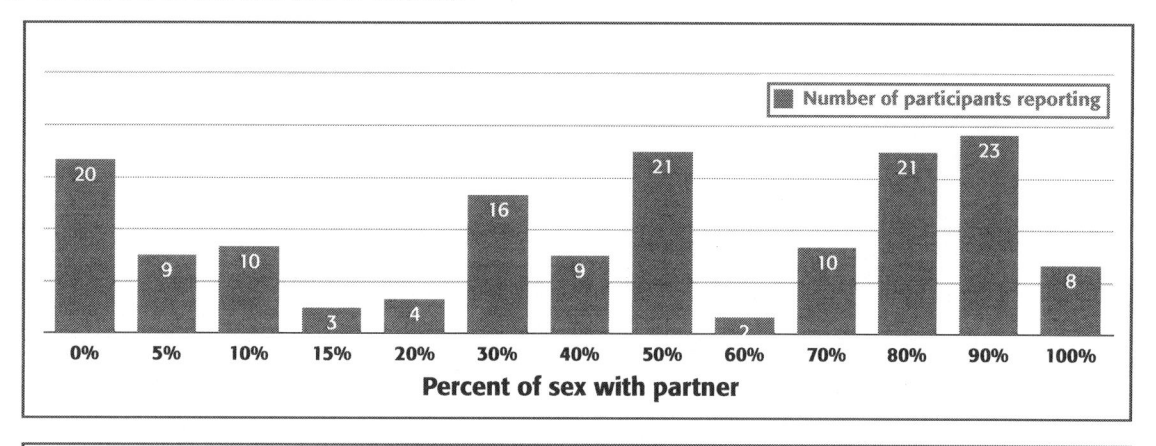

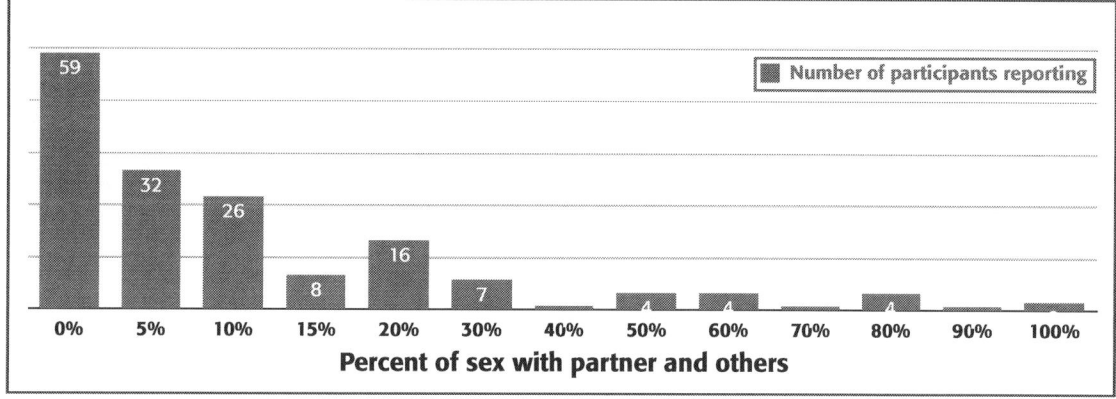

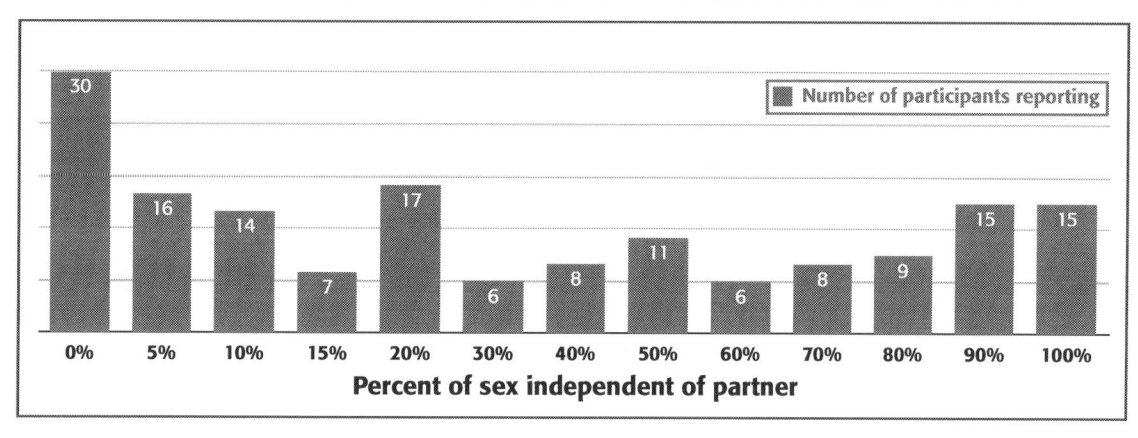

Percent of sex with partner (Number of participants reporting):
0%	5%	10%	15%	20%	30%	40%	50%	60%	70%	80%	90%	100%
20	9	10	3	4	16	9	21	2	10	21	23	8

Percent of sex with partner and others (Number of participants reporting):
0%	5%	10%	15%	20%	30%	40%	50%	60%	70%	80%	90%	100%
59	32	26	8	16	7		4	4		4		

Percent of sex independent of partner (Number of participants reporting):
0%	5%	10%	15%	20%	30%	40%	50%	60%	70%	80%	90%	100%
30	16	14	7	17	6	8	11	6	8	9	15	15

Love without sex

Study couples fell into four clusters in terms of their own sex lives. 15% were couples who no longer had sex together, but still felt very close, loving and connected to each other. One of the biggest learnings for us as authors was to hear couples in this group glowingly talk about their relationship. Prior to the study, we imagined couples whose own sex lives had dwindled were more like room-mates. Repeatedly, we listened to partners talk about their affection and concern for each other, their joy in companionship, their loyalty and commitment. It was quite gratifying to let go of our misperception and we noticed this was the one study finding we most enjoyed sharing when asked what we were learning.

Most of these couples seemed quite comfortable with having let go of their sex lives together. It was shared rather matter of factly – been there, done that and moved on. The 'routineness' of many years with the same person was a leading cause, but some couples acknowledged their early sex lives together had never been terribly passionate or compatible. In other cases, it was more one-sided with one partner having health issues and/or losing interest in sex altogether. A few participants described their own pattern of becoming bored with any partner after a certain amount of time.

Rather than lamenting the lost sex life together, the couples in this cluster focused on the strength and joy in their relationship and were pleased that their open relationship allowed them to carry on as sexual beings without giving up what they most valued. The outside sex for these couples was most often anonymous and characterized as a necessary response to a physical drive. Although it was important not to squelch their sex drive, it was deemed rather insignificant when compared to what they valued in their relationship.

> We haven't had much sex together in the last few years, but we're very, very affectionate. We hug, kiss and cuddle all the time. With every encounter, we say we love each other and let the other one know they look great.

> Sex is about chemistry. It either works or it doesn't. Our chemistry has been pretty average from the beginning. He's attractive – even more so, now. But he's very vanilla. Outside sex keeps us from wandering. If you can scratch an itch, it feels better, and sometimes that's all it takes. If the sex doesn't work out, do you throw away the rest of the relationship? We threw out the sex and kept the relationship.

> Our relationship is now non-sexual, and has been so for 5 years. Our relationship has never really been about sex. Jim would like a bottom, but I don't bottom. And Jim NEVER bottoms, so we're a non-match. We kiss a lot, tell each other we love the other, and hold hands. Outside sex has allowed us to stay together because it isn't a point of contention.

> We no longer have sex together. It's been about six years. I'm not a particularly sexual person. I always lose interest and there are many things I'd rather be doing than having sex. I used to worry about what am I not doing right, but I'm comfortable with who I am. We don't have sex, but I don't feel like we've lost anything in the relationship.

> I haven't had sex in the last three years with Brad, and not with anyone outside for two years. I don't need outside sex and I have a high level of affection, cuddling, kissing, with Brad that I find very satisfying. He still goes out and I want him to. I don't know if it's physical or emotional, but I just don't have the urge.

> I used to feel that things weren't okay with us unless we were having sex. But we have committed to always be together and I trust that. Now, I know it's okay to not be having sex together – our relationship is much more than just sex.

I focus on the good we have. We keep affirming that we love each other and that we want to be together. We don't take each other for granted. When my brother was killed, Allan stepped in and took care of all of us, including my Mom. That's the way he shows me he loves me.

Sex isn't what keeps us together. Sex is a minor thing. I just cherish him and his qualities. He constantly keeps me interested.

What makes us partners if we don't have sex together? In my mind, we're lifetime partners. I can't imagine feeling the way I do about him with anyone else.

On the wane

10% of couples characterized their sex lives as increasingly infrequent or on the wane. Unlike the first group, some of these couples did express a sense of loss, particularly if one partner was still interested (and the other wasn't). Others seemed ambivalent. They wished it was more frequent, but didn't have the energy or the inclination to make it a focus. As with the first cluster, these couples put their emphasis on what they loved and valued about their partner and their relationship.

We don't have as much sex together now, which I would want and we probably go out more. I'm not sure what we can do about that. It changed at some point and we talk about it. We probably aren't working as hard to have sex with each other because we can go out. This isn't the cause of why we're not having that much sex together, but it does lessen the motivation to work on it. Of course, saying we would be monogamous at all costs would be much more negative.

We love each other; we kiss everyday; we snuggle at night. As we age, sex becomes less and less a primary drive. I'm really glad we have everything else together and didn't lose it because of sex.

I am at a place now where I'd much rather have sex with my husband, than anyone else. I don't like the idea of a sexless marriage. It makes me feel old. Love is spiritual. I'm sad that we don't have more drive toward each other.

We just don't fit together sexually. We keep trying. I wish we had it, but it's okay with me that we don't. I wonder if being able to go outside is an easy way out of working on our own sexual intimacy. I hadn't really thought about it until now. But obviously we haven't been very motivated – it may solely be a 'should' from society that we should be having sex together.

We don't have sex. He told me the numbers he gave you and I laughed. I guess he still has some Gloria Vanderbilt notion of what we should be.

We're so much in love with each other, but we know that we have separate sexual interests. We each have guys we trust that we can play with from time to time. But I know what I have in Devon and I really value it. We have the same core values about family, money, interests in people - the things that really matter.

In my last relationship we were monogamous and after 7 years, we had no sex. Having this one be open, I don't have to worry about that happening. As the amount of sex we have together goes down, that won't be a reason for us to break up. It means we will still be able to have outside sex and stay together. It's reassuring.

Fanning the fire

30% of couples were still quite engaged with each other sexually although they expressed concerns about how to keep this alive. Many couples in this group used outside sex to energize their own sex together. Whether by sharing titillating details, experimenting with newly learned techniques, or playing together with outsiders, outside sex was seen as a helpful contributor to keeping their own sex life vibrant. Some couples described having date nights and deliberately setting time aside – making sure it was a priority.

I didn't want to become roommates. I always kept that in the back of my mind. We got into porn movies; that was stimulating. When I go to The Club, I usually don't get off and so I fuck Barry the next morning. Going out seems to stir things up. We have one couple we play with who never cum with us, but save it for when they go home together.

We realized we're both still attractive and that makes us more attractive to each other – we still have something to offer each other. We had become complacent about our sex life. We were always busy with other things and never made the time. We're much more sexual with each other now.

Terry says he doesn't care how much I get on the outside as long as he's getting some with me. I make a point to make sure he's getting enough. Periodically, I reassess myself. Am I withholding? Am I going outside, instead of having sex with Terry? Is going out tonight good for us?

I am sometimes regretful that I find it so pleasurable to find sex outside the relationship. I wish we could find all the amusement we needed within the relationship. I don't attach any value to monogamy, so it's not about that. You'd think having the man of my dreams would be enough. We do make date nights. I'm on a medication that affects my erections. If I can't do it, I want him to get his needs met and to feel good. I have no qualms about that. We had a guy give him a superb time – that was hot as all hell for me.

We both have had previous relationships. We know we have to focus on each other and the relationship. Gene would probably want more sex since his libido is higher than mine. We know we have to take time away from our stress and work-lives and spend quality time. We set up date nights. I also know it's more important to me to have the experience with Gene than alone. I've done the other.

What's Libido Got to Do With It?

We had participants rate their libido on a scale of 1 (low) to 10 (high). The average libido of study participants was 7. We didn't find any important patterns related to libido, but we will share a few observations:

- Our average would be much higher if we included the frequent responses of '11', '12', and 'off the charts' (we scored these as 10's).
- Most participants' libidos were quite similar to the libido of their partner.
- A few participants reported very low libidos, which certainly had an impact on how invested they were in any type of sex. For some, having their partner be able to go out was a relief.
- Although a few commented on their libidos declining as they aged, many participants in their 60's and older reported strong libidos.
- A few related a great deal of fluctuation in their libidos due to steroids, aging or HIV

Still vibrant

The remaining couples (45%) had active sex lives together and a) either made positive comments about this, or b) didn't express concerns. Other than these two criteria, there is no clear distinction between this group and the previous cluster. Couples in both clusters are apt to be 'fanning the fire'.

What's important here is the number of long-term couples that are still quite sexually active with each other. On average, the couples in this cluster had been together 15.3 years, with 6 of these couples having 20+ years together. When combined with the previous cluster, 75% of study couples continued to have active sex lives with each other.

We asked some of the couples who had been together the longest if they had thoughts about what fueled and sustained their sex lives together. Some said sex together had always been a central driving focus. Many related having a fair amount of outside sex with much of it together. Switching roles, high compatibility, a deepening sense of trust, and an appreciation of the ease and intimacy were also offered as contributing factors. A few of these couples noted that their interest in outside sex was waning. Hooking up with others required too much effort and they were finding themselves increasingly content and fulfilled playing at home.

> We're both in our 50's and we're becoming insatiable again, but it's mostly with each other. We're closer to monogamy than we were.

> It's enhanced our relationship, particularly sexually. We still have sex together after 20 years and it probably wouldn't be as frequent or as passionate. If we were monogamous, we would have bottled up our frustration and I'm 99% sure we'd be doing stuff behind each other's back.

> We are more relaxed with each other and we have seen each other in every light possible - seeing all sides of each other. We learned a lot sexually by going out and we added to our sex play together. We've become more appreciative of each other and what we have.

> Initially opening the relationship damaged our own sex life. We got excited about the three ways and found that we were saving ourselves for the weekend when we would go out together looking for a third. We weren't having as much sex with each other. I brought it to Mac's attention and said it wasn't okay - we had to put as much energy into our own sex life. We talked about it and made a point to focus on it. At this point, having outside sex has improved our sex life together. We've brought back ideas and techniques and energy and brought it back into the relationship.

Rob

It's made our own sex life better. I don't see how you can stay together and still have a great sex life without having 'outside' inspiration. Your body ages and the libido may vary, so it's a matter of keeping the interest alive. We work to make sex beautiful and interesting. It puts you in a good mind-set and makes it something to look forward to. I would really miss it if we stopped.

John:

I find that if things are getting stale, going out together for a 3-some or a party will bring Rob and me closer. I never have a problem with sex; I see it as integral. Rob has ups and downs in terms of his sexual libido. Outside involvement encourages Rob to be more sexual.

What's the Impact? Benefits & Risks

We asked couples to describe the impact outside sex had on their relationship. We were careful to position this question neutrally, without pulling for positives or negatives. If there seemed to be any confusion, we always clarified by saying "we were looking for both positive and negative impact". In the case of participants who had an immediate response of "Nothing has been negative" (end of conversation), we did ask if there had been any positive impact.

Both positive and negative impact

21% of participants shared both positives and negatives in their responses. The quotes below give a perspective of the trade-offs. Notice how many of the benefits go beyond 'just providing a sexual outlet'. And these benefits come with some risk.

✔ Makes relationship more interesting, in general. We're not closed; we're open – so we're meeting new people and that enriches what we bring to the relationship. It forces us to be more honest. It helps us be more willing and comfortable to talk about what might be difficult.

✘ There's people you can't talk to (family and friends) about being non-monogamous. We stopped having sex together a few years ago. Occasionally we do three ways. So that leaves me wondering "Would we have tried harder to make our sex life work together if it were the only option?"

✔ It's created adventure and it's allowed us to join together in playfulness. It encourages us to talk about our feelings and it serves as a catalyst for new perspectives into our relationship. It challenges trust, but on the other hand it helps us hone our sense of trust. If we can navigate it well, we can be more trusting.

✘ In addition to the tension, I worry that it means our relationship is aberrant. There's no clear model and so we don't know if we're doing the right thing or how to do the right thing. And there is stigma to going outside the relationship.

✔ It's helped us evolve. We feel we really want to be together. We've learned that we can trust each other. Ted can go out clubbing and I decided that I could either trust him or not and I realized I clearly trust him. We have better communication because we have talked about outside sex and how to handle it.

✘ The only negative is we have more worries about getting a disease.

✔ It's underscored the importance of honesty in the relationship. It's forced us to be more intentional in how we navigate and evolve the relationship. It's helped increase our communication muscles.

✘ It's brought some pain and confusion and it's required a certain amount of expenditure of energy.

✓ We're probably more relaxed with each other – sex isn't as charged.

✗ It's taken some emphasis off our one-on-one sex. Its spread the focus a little wider and now we're not totally dependent on each other for sex. After a 3-way, sex together is very nice and sometimes it feels less exciting.

✓ It's allowed the relationship to survive. It's brought more honesty and openness to the relationship. We're both reassured about the relationship continuing. We've got several fuck buddies with whom we've become good friends.

✗ There are still moments of jealousy.

✓ It's improved our sex lives both internally (with each other) and externally. We're both more sexually satisfied. It's kept my sex drive going.

✗ The downside is there have been some hurt feelings; I feel distrusted; and there's been a few traumatic situations.

Randy:

✓ I got sexually bored. I also wanted outside validation – "I know Art thinks I'm hot, but I wanted a second opinion." Art also didn't think he was that attractive and so I wanted him to experience that others perceived him similarly to me. He finally opened up to noticing others and their response to him. It was a joy for me to see.

✗ It has introduced something in our relationship that we can't do together. I'm missing him. We also now have 'secrets' from others since we don't tell family and friends.

Art:

✓ I really enjoy the outside sex, so in some ways, it strengthens the relationship. It's a blessing that we can be open so that we can stay together and not be sexually frustrated and biting at each other.

✗ Randy and I are pretty tight emotionally, but being open to outside sex has diminished that a bit. There's a bit of the pie chart missing. There are people outside the relationship with whom we're being intimate and we're not sharing that as it happens. I regret that.

Primarily negative impact

A few participants (4%) shared strong negatives. This was more apt to be the case for couples where the decision to be open or closed is still not fully resolved.

✖ It's brought issues of insensitivity and lack of confidence to the fore. It's allowed me to observe both our behaviors. The issues would be there anyway, but they get exacerbated by sex. We get competitive around sex.

✖ It hasn't always gone well. There have been a lot of hurt feelings and arguments. It's been one of the more difficult aspects of our relationship. However, we both believe that sex is very important. I don't believe any one person can meet all of your sexual needs. So, we keep coming back to outside sex and we're getting better about communicating. We do really care for each other.

Todd:

✖ Outside sex has really gotten in the way of the relationship because it's caused conflict. On the other hand, I don't think I could stay in the relationship if it wasn't allowed to continue. Although maybe I would find that I could.

Ron:

✖ It's had a destructive impact. It's been problematic and has caused a lot of hurt on both sides. It's diminished our relationship and has been hard on both of us. During the times when outside sex has worked, I've found it enriching and it has recharged my sexual appetite with Todd.

Connor:

✖ It's brought a real negative to our sex life because of the fear of disease. There's more tension. It definitely feels like something has been lost, due to trust and lack of intimacy. We discuss it but there are still things to work out.

Logan:

✖ It's been hurtful. It's caused distrust. I haven't regained my trust in Connor yet, although some of that is about the way we went about it and the way I found out.

Positive impact

The vast majority (75%) of responses were solely positive. We would expect a fairly strong endorsement given participants' self-selection into the study. It's not surprising to us that participants appreciate having a sanctioned sexual outlet. What is striking is the number of benefits beyond having a sexual outlet that participants shared. These included greater communication, increased trust and openness between partners, and the opportunity for individuals to explore and meet individual needs.

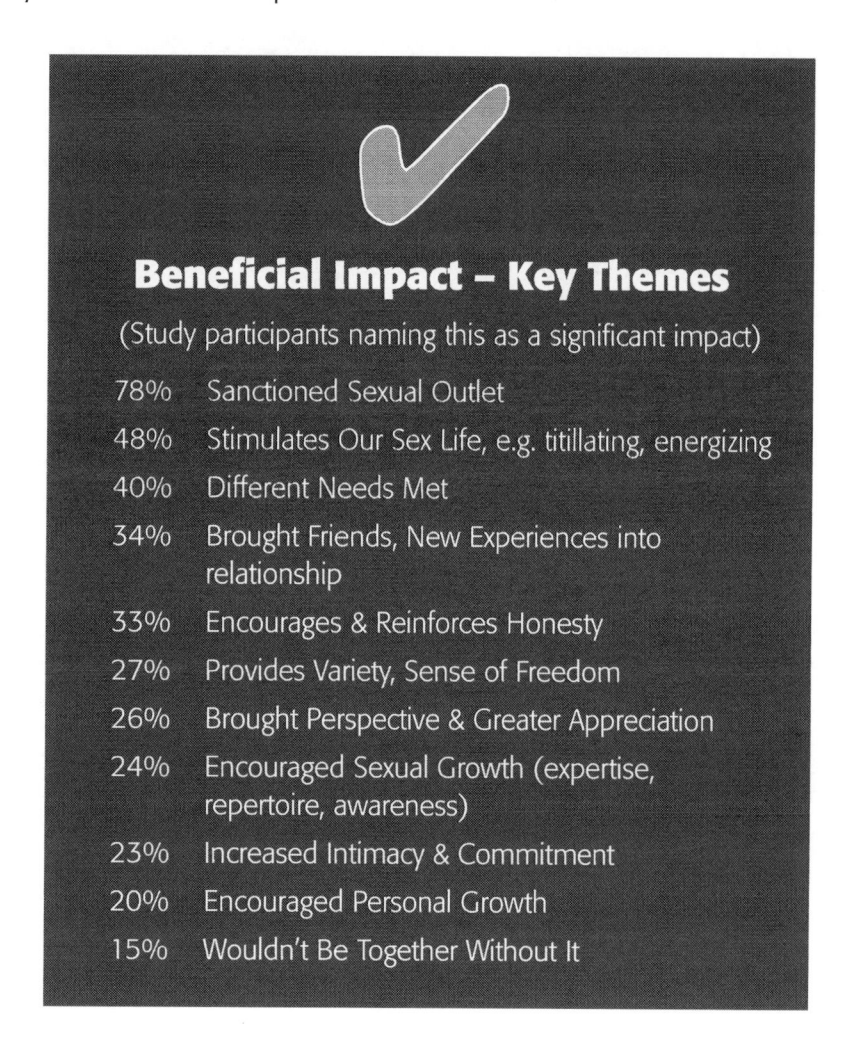

Beneficial Impact – Key Themes
(Study participants naming this as a significant impact)

%	Theme
78%	Sanctioned Sexual Outlet
48%	Stimulates Our Sex Life, e.g. titillating, energizing
40%	Different Needs Met
34%	Brought Friends, New Experiences into relationship
33%	Encourages & Reinforces Honesty
27%	Provides Variety, Sense of Freedom
26%	Brought Perspective & Greater Appreciation
24%	Encouraged Sexual Growth (expertise, repertoire, awareness)
23%	Increased Intimacy & Commitment
20%	Encouraged Personal Growth
15%	Wouldn't Be Together Without It

Sanctioned sexual outlet

The first theme was the most basic. Overtly and consciously opening up the relationship, allows couples to pursue outside sex without being deceitful. 78% of the study participants named this as a significant impact.

Having an open relationship is much more satisfying. I hated the pattern of sneaking around – it's a demeaning way to live. If you're not satisfied being monogamous, it's much more healthy psychologically to be open. Having a 'secret life' is tough on everybody – yourself, your partner, and those with whom you play.

It's just sex. It's an outlet. It's neither positive nor negative. But it's important that it's honest.

Having it open works for us. It's way better than lying about it. Thinking it won't happen is a recipe for disaster. We're men. It's like "You really don't expect me not to get a blow job when I need one, do you?"

It takes so much of the worry and the stress and the jealousy away from the relationship. It makes the relationship so enjoyable. It's been awesome.

Sex is really important. I would not have had a happy life if I had tried to damp down that part of my life to be a dutiful little housewife. We both require a lot of sex with a lot of men and we both like it so we have to give each other space. It's just an element of our lives. The fact that it works reinforces it.

It's been a good thing. It keeps things exciting sexually. We still have good sex together after 12 years. We've made some good friends. If we were monogamous, I'd be cheating for sure and if I wasn't, I'd become resentful over time. I'd be resentful of the lack of trust - that I couldn't be trusted to see someone only once. That's what happened in my last relationship.

It's made it much easier for me to handle being away from each other. It would have been hard not having any sex – I have a high libido. It's helped me want to sustain the relationship even though we're separated at times.

It's made us much stronger. It's eliminated the arguing and worrying and tension that there's going to be someone else down the road. It's basically not an arguing point. It takes the pressure off of us sexually, especially when I'm travelling. It makes our other time together that much more precious.

Being open about outside sex makes it so much more comfortable. There's no tension and stress of 'playing the game' of being monogamous. It's been very refreshing. I know he's going to be there for me and so I can play around. I saw him making out with a guy at a party. It was awkward, but I didn't feel jealous because I knew he was going home with me.

Men are wired to like variety and differences. It's an acknowledgement of how we're wired sexually that we can go out together. We have an outlet for this with clear boundaries that allows us to meet those needs honestly and cleanly.

It eliminates the dishonesty and allows us to follow our natural inclinations. I don't think it affects our emotional intimacy. We're avoiding the deceit, mistrust and drama that sometimes comes with this territory.

Stimulates our sex life

48% of study participants shared that having outside sex was helpful to the couples' own sex life. We discussed aspects of this earlier in the sections on Integration and Couples' Own Sex Lives. Here are a few more examples:

> It supplements are own sex life. It adds variety. We're sexual beings and it allows for that. It's an ego boost – others still find me attractive. It makes me proud when others find Robert attractive. "He's my man, so that's an ego boost as well.

> When you're as horny and provocative as we are, there has to be a sexual outlet. It serves as a release valve. It's not the most important part of our relationship. We have sex together once or twice a week. If I didn't have sex with Gary alone, why would I want to share him with a third? But the outside sex helps break up the patterns that get established and it adds to our repertoire. We often talk about three-ways during sex. We sometimes watch our own movies (with others), while we have sex. If anything it strengthens our relationship.

> It helps our sex life to have outside sex. Usually after we're done playing with someone, we end up playing with each other. It turns us on a lot.

> It's made the relationship more honest and strong and sometimes livelier. We're not bored with sex. We're not going behind each other's backs. We enjoy playing together. It's above board. It validates how strong the relationship is and after 20 years, you need a little diversity to stoke your interest.

> It's improved our sex life. A few years ago, I wasn't as excited at home. I'm not into anonymous sex so our sex life matters. I'm more interested in sex than I would be at this point in my life and it breaks us out of our sexual routines and patterns. We bring new options back.

> It makes me happy to see him have a smile on his face. He draws me in and it draws us closer. We're aroused with each other after we've gone out. I'm astounded by how many people comment on how happy we are around each other. They're surprised at how light-hearted we are together. They ask, "Don't you ever get tired of each other?' But we don't.

> I've learned more about John's sexual needs and I would never have found out, which means I might never have satisfied him sexually. Going outside augments my need for sex. For both of us, it increases our own self image and confidence. It's fun. It brings more overall sexual satisfaction into my life. It's made us stronger and will continue to make us stronger. I wish we would both have more outside sex. Neither of us is very impulsive.

Stimulates our sex life

48% of study participants shared that having outside sex was helpful to the couples' own sex life. We discussed aspects of this earlier in the sections on Integration and Couples' Own Sex Lives. Here are a few more examples:

It supplements are own sex life. It adds variety. We're sexual beings and it allows for that. It's an ego boost – others still find me attractive. It makes me proud when others find Robert attractive. "He's my man, so that's an ego boost as well.

When you're as horny and provocative as we are, there has to be a sexual outlet. It serves as a release valve. It's not the most important part of our relationship. We have sex together once or twice a week. If I didn't have sex with Gary alone, why would I want to share him with a third? But the outside sex helps break up the patterns that get established and it adds to our repertoire. We often talk about three-ways during sex. We sometimes watch our own movies (with others), while we have sex. If anything it strengthens our relationship.

It helps our sex life to have outside sex. Usually after we're done playing with someone, we end up playing with each other. It turns us on a lot.

It's made the relationship more honest and strong and sometimes livelier. We're not bored with sex. We're not going behind each other's backs. We enjoy playing together. It's above board. It validates how strong the relationship is and after 20 years, you need a little diversity to stoke your interest.

It's improved our sex life. A few years ago, I wasn't as excited at home. I'm not into anonymous sex so our sex life matters. I'm more interested in sex than I would be at this point in my life and it breaks us out of our sexual routines and patterns. We bring new options back.

It makes me happy to see him have a smile on his face. He draws me in and it draws us closer. We're aroused with each other after we've gone out. I'm astounded by how many people comment on how happy we are around each other. They're surprised at how light-hearted we are together. They ask, "Don't you ever get tired of each other?' But we don't.

I've learned more about John's sexual needs and I would never have found out, which means I might never have satisfied him sexually. Going outside augments my need for sex. For both of us, it increases our own self image and confidence. It's fun. It brings more overall sexual satisfaction into my life. It's made us stronger and will continue to make us stronger. I wish we would both have more outside sex. Neither of us is very impulsive.

Will's roving libido has been difficult. But it also brought people and experiences into our relationship. Morris was an amazing person. I wouldn't have been at the sex party last weekend and had a fabulously good time if Morris hadn't entered our lives. More importantly, Morris was able to instruct Will about the importance of playing safely. Will couldn't hear that from me.

The reason I wanted an open relationship is because I was exploring S/M and the leather world. It wasn't having sex per se, but I wanted to be able to get naked and experiment. It became a big part of both our identities for a number of years. We got better at communication because of the outside leather sex. We learned to say what we want and don't want, to set limits and to respect boundaries.

We've got some really good friends we have sex with and we've met really neat people through them. It's widened our circle.

Encourages and reinforces honesty

A certain degree of honesty is prerequisite for having an explicit agreement about outside sex. And for the agreement to work, on-going candor is required. 33% reported that having an open relationship encouraged honest conversation about attractions, fears, insecurities, desires – all of which might be easier to not acknowledge.

It's made us honest with each other. We're doing what we want. If we weren't honest about what we wanted, my head would explode.

It's also created a much more honest and trusting environment. Our communication has improved tremendously. We say what we really feel and are comfortable doing it.

It has caused us to look at ourselves and our relationship in a more honest and real way. If we can be honest about this, it makes other stuff easier to be honest about.

Because we opened up the relationship, it makes it stronger. The honesty that's required strengthens our relationship. We've learned to be honest about our needs and to talk more openly about desires toward others without taking offense.

One couple we spoke with waited 24 years before addressing the fact that they were both going out. They described it as a watershed moment and when we spoke with them two years later, they were still excited about how this had changed their interactions. They found themselves being much more honest and open with each other - not only about sex, but also in sharing their respective inner experiences – thoughts, feelings, goals. This level of sharing was new to them and encouraged a much greater intimacy.

It was romantic and monogamous at the beginning. Then we fell into having outside sex, but neither of us ever talked about it. A couple of years ago, we decided to be brutally honest with each other. It's improved because we never used to talk about anything. Now we talk more as individuals. Advice I would give to a new couple: It's better to be honest from the start and just accept someone. Sit down and put your cards on the table. Talk about what you need and don't pretend. Start now, rather than wait 26 years. It's a very freeing experience. When it's not in the open, you know something is happening in the shadows and that's what fuels the insecurity and jealously. You have to realize you can't meet all your partner's needs – you have to meet your own needs.

Provides variety, sense of freedom

27% of participants valued the sense of freedom and/or the variety going outside offered:

> I still find Charles very attractive and we have plenty of sex together, but it would have been hard for me not to have sex with anyone else. I would have felt trapped. It would have been like a prison. I would have been able to comply, but I would have been resentful – like there was something out there I wasn't getting to experience.

> It's been positive. Although we are devoted to each other, we want to maintain our individuality. It gives us some freedom. We don't want one person to be controlling or dominant. And this goes along with not limiting the other person. Love is about opening up to someone, not controlling them.

> It's given us a release valve. Having a life partner doesn't necessitate denying the desire for others. By having permission, you recognize the desire and work together with your partner to accommodate outside sex in a way that is respectful to each other. By having a release valve, it allows us to be closer. It's also helped us loosen some inhibitions.

> It gave us wiggle room. Wiggle room to have a little bit of freedom and not be solely dependent on each other.

> Having the option to play has allowed us to not feel trapped or caged in the relationship. We haven't had to feel limited or give up the possibility of ever going out. Clark doesn't want to feel controlled or on a leash and this gives him a sense of freedom. And that's true for both of us.

> We like variety. I love sex with Will and love making love to Will, but I also like variety. It spices up our sex life.

> It relieves frustration. If I'm in a rut, I can go get laid and come home happy. If I come home happy, it helps the relationship. Letting Robert have outside sex makes him bearable. He's so intense; it makes him easier to be with.

> On my night out, after outside sex, I can't wait to come home and sleep with Robert.

Brought perspective and greater appreciation

26% of participants talked about the perspective that going outside has brought.

> It's helped me realize that there are many aspects to relationship and sex isn't and shouldn't be the primary aspect. Sex may be a relatively minor element in some primary relationships.

> I learn a lot by contrasts. Going outside makes me realize what I have in my relationship. Over the years, it's allowed me to see aspects of our relationship and the whole of our relationship and where sex fits in. It's no longer the forbidden fruit.

> On the whole it's been positive. We handle each other better. We learned to ask each other more questions – to pull each other out. It carried over beyond sex. We became more aware of each other's needs and became more sensitive. Over the years it helped us appreciate each other more. Sometimes fucking someone else just put things in perspective. Coming home to Dennis was the best thing of the evening.

> It continues to strengthen our bond and our appreciation of each other.

> It has a positive effect. It adds some life to things; takes you outside the ordinary. It brings variety — like going on vacation. It makes me appreciate the sex and the relationship I have with Max.

> It makes us realize the grass is no greener.

> It makes us appreciate our relationship, physically and emotionally. It keeps us from being distracted by others. It's a release valve. If it wasn't open, we'd probably both be cheating.

Encouraged sexual growth

24% of participants acknowledged growing sexually as a result of outside experiences. This included increasing their expertise, repertoire and sense of sexuality.

> It's helped me become less repressed. I feel like I'm healthier sexually - I'm more relaxed, adventuresome and happier.

> Over time it allowed us to experiment and evolve sexually. I was a total top and I've become more versatile.

> It's allowed us to be honest about who we are and what we want.

> I used it as an opportunity to explore what I had always fantasized about – BDSM. I've learned about myself. I've had a lot of interesting experiences that I wouldn't have had otherwise.

> It's made me more aware of my body and my own sexuality. Outside sex is a healthy thing for us and doesn't have any downsides. It has led to our growth as individuals and to the growth of our relationship.

> I like to get to walk the world as a sexual being. I like that I haven't had to give that up. Having outside sex and the possibility of outside sex brings excitement.

> I'm more comfortable with my sexuality. I had never been to a sex club before. We've gone twice. Once was really good and once was really boring. I don't have any judgments about that kind of thing now. I did before. I'll try new things and I have freedom and also a sense of relief.

Increased intimacy and commitment

23% of participants spoke specifically about intimacy and about the relationship becoming stronger.

> It's allowed a deeper intimacy and a deeper relationship. To really be this open requires an enormous amount of integrity, self-confidence and deep honesty. Our experience of having this freedom is indicative of a healthy relationship, not unhealthy. Friends often don't understand the depth of our love and the depth of the relationship because they see us going out and think that somehow means we care less.

> It has helped solidify our relationship. It prompted deeper conversations than we even knew we were prepared to have. It required more sharing at a deeper level.

It encourages us to be more honest about our thoughts and feelings. We're closer with each other. I'm more willing to share 100% of myself with him and there's much less 'mine/yours' & more 'ours'. I find myself more generous – even with finances. I think that's because there's greater trust and I'm happier about the relationship so I want to be more generous.

It's another step on the ladder, another defining point of our commitment. Something we can do together and enjoy doing together that has built our relationship further and made it stronger.

It's enhanced our intimacy. We can have variety by going outside, but it makes me appreciate what we have at home. I equate it to filet mignon. I want to have rib or sirloin, but when I do it makes me appreciate I have filet mignon at home. It's reassuring to be desired. It helps my self-esteem. We're still sexual, a part of the community, feel vital.

We currently have a beautiful man we've taken under our wing. It keeps that fire burning in us. It's amazing how life can open up and what the universe has to show us when you're as connected and in love as we are.

Encouraged personal growth

20% talked more generally about how they had grown personally as a result of outside sexual experiences.

It's created better dynamics in our relationship. I'm more honest with my emotions and able to communicate them. Tom is more self-aware and able to acknowledge that he's made a mistake. He would never have said he was sorry before. I would not have expected it, but being open is far better than it was before. It's made me more in touch with Tom and made me a better person.

We're both on different paths and learning new things. We share with each other what we've learned and we experience the ways each of us has grown. I think eventually we will come back and be more focused on each other sexually with everything we have learned. I would like that and want that . It's made us continually define our relationship – which keeps it alive and growing.

I've asserted myself more in the relationship as a result of having to stick up for the 'rules'. Friends tell me how much I've changed. It's caused us to be much more open and honest.

If we hadn't opened the relationship, I wouldn't have found S/M and that let me grow and become more confident. And my ability to express it and have James support it and support me, increased our intimacy together. James was encouraging and non-judgmental. It's brought us closer.

It's been transformative, although it's a constant balancing and juggling. I've discovered things about myself. I've become connected to new people. It's opened me to new worlds. It's not all positive, but it's made me wiser and I understand that relationships can operate on multiple levels.

It makes us more loving toward each other. It's like exercise. When I'm with someone I'm practicing being loving and I bring it back. The more love I give away the more I have to give.

Outside sex has helped me grow as a person – psychologically, spiritually and lovingly.

Wouldn't be together without it

15% of participants responded rather matter-of-factly that they wouldn't be together without it. This comment was offered in two ways. Some participants felt outside sex was essential and they couldn't imagine going without. Others felt their relationship was essential and they were glad that the lack of sex at home was not a deal-breaker.

> It's allowed us to stay together in a great relationship, even though we're not sexually very compatible. If we didn't go out, we'd get frustrated. I'm certain we would break up.

> If it hadn't been open, our relationship wouldn't have become long-term. I like variety. "I love you, but there's lots of men out there." Barry is more nurturing and wouldn't have needed outside sex. I needed a long leash and this relationship allowed that.

> It has kept us together. I don't want to be celibate or have severe limitations. I'm glad that there are alternatives and I can get my needs met without threatening the relationship.

> The relationship wouldn't have survived without it. We like sex with other guys. It's something we both really enjoy. I love to watch him with someone and he loves to watch me with someone. We don't have sex with just each other that much - maybe once a month. We like to have others involved.

Discussion of Results

Providing a descriptive picture of what non-monogamy looks like was a core aim of this study. Because of this, we've stayed very close to the data, providing concrete examples and avoiding speculation. When we step back and look more generally at the study findings, the conclusions we draw are more sweeping.

A viable option

We assume we had a study population skewed towards the positive, but nonetheless, it is reasonable to conclude that non-monogamy for gay male couples is a viable option. When partners find enough common ground in their inclinations and perspectives toward non-monogamy, sanctioned outside sex is a sustainable and satisfying possibility.

If a couple is willing to be forthright and to problem-solve as needed, non-monogamy isn't by nature de-stabilizing. In fact, the results of this study would suggest the opposite – many study couples said non-monogamy enabled them to stay together. The average length of relationship for interviewed couples was 16 years – double our minimum requirement. Given the difficulties we had in recruiting participants, this figure suggests a positive correlation between longevity and non-monogamy. At a minimum, it destroys the myth that opening the relationship is the 'beginning of the end'.

The study also counters a second, and corollary, myth: open relationships are somehow less – less healthy, less loving, less responsible. Again, the results of this study would suggest quite the opposite. Certainly, non-monogamous couples can be as dysfunctional as monogamous couples, but they can also be as nurturing, trusting and cohesive. The vast majority of our study couples appeared to have caring, loving, and healthy partnerships.

What's the payoff?

We found many couples had a somewhat compartmentalized perspective and approach to outside sex. "It's just sex" – a release without meaning, quite separate from the relationship. For these couples, non-monogamy offers a valuable and satisfying outlet that's sanctioned and acknowledged. It allows men to 'follow their nature', meet differing needs, and seek variety without jeopardizing their relationship.

A majority of study couples had a more integrative approach to non-monogamy. There was less anonymity and more personal connection with outside sex partners, more sharing of information and discussion of what got stirred up, and an effort to bring back and utilize the energy and lessons of the outside experience for the betterment of the relationship. For these couples, non-monogamy brought additional benefits beyond the sexual outlet. Couples spoke of greater trust, more forthright communication, personal growth, increased perspective, and more drive in their own sex lives together.

What's the catch?

Some couples experienced non-monogamy as a 'no-brainer'. They found an approach that worked for them with little difficulty or fanfare. This was more likely to be the case if outside sex was agreed upon at the beginning of the relationship and they had a compartmentalizing approach to outside sex.

However, for most couples, there was a price of admission. Non-monogamy came with risks and required maintenance. It may trigger uncomfortable feelings; it may provoke disagreements and tension, it may require self-reflection and personal growth, it may necessitate changing how a couple communicates and interacts. This was especially true for couples that valued sharing and integrating the experiences of non-monogamy. We also suspect this might be more likely for couples in the general population – couples who might be reluctant to participate in a study.

Couples have to decide what will work for them and how they can best minimize and navigate the risks. There isn't a simple model to follow. Couples don't know ahead of time what will surface or what will be required. They may be challenged by any, and probably many, of the following:

- clarifying values and making certain they are mutual,
- appreciating and accommodating differences,
- holding steadfast to agreements and a commitment to honesty,
- growing greater capacity to process and manage their own emotional reactions
- learning to voice their desires, concerns, and uncomfortable feelings
- becoming increasingly vulnerable, trusting, forgiving, generous
- partnering to constructively problem-solve and find resolution for unforeseen and possibly highly charged issues

It's an intriguing list - not advised for the faint-hearted, yet full of possibilities for individual and relationship growth. As one study participant said, "Both people have to want it bad enough to be willing to pay the price and do the work required."

What is enough communication?

Many couples mentioned that communication was critical. Some couples were very self-reflective and very verbal in their processing. Some couples were deeply in tune with each other and preferred finding their way intuitively. In between were couples that seemed more sporadic or 'hit and miss' in their communication with each other. We were surprised at the number of times we heard, "Mmmm, we've never discussed that." Or "That's an interesting question, I never really thought about that."

We found ourselves wondering and sometimes worrying about these couples. When they took the initiative to communicate, it worked well for them. But they often defaulted to making assumptions without confirming them with their partner. If the assumptions they made proved to be correct (and they often did), they were home free.

But we began to question if the study had a preponderance of 'couples who were lucky'. In the larger population would we see more couples with this approach that had 'guessed wrong'? We certainly heard from some study couples who paid heavily for a previous lack of communication or proactive consideration. We're speculating here, but if a couple wants to minimize the risks inherent in non-monogamy, it seems best to err on the side of checking out assumptions and inquiring into perspectives.

Dealing with differences

The study couples most likely to struggle were ones that were challenged by core differences. Certainly the most difficult situation was when partners differed in their desire to open the relationship. Until they could come to some shared agreement about what they both wanted, couples typically experienced recurring tension and frustration. We assume this is much more prevalent in the larger population which includes couples reluctant to participate in a study.

Another common area of difficulty was partners who had differing preferences for connection. It took partners time to realize the difference and to recognize the innate character of this difference. Initially there's the assumption - "He thinks like me." After a bit of discovery this becomes, "Why doesn't he think like me?" Unfortunately, accommodation and resolution only become possible when there is recognition that both perspectives are valid. At that point partners can shift to "What will we need from each other to make this work?" – a much more fruitful question to be asking.

There are myriad sources of difference that can prove to be problematic. Partners may have strong differences in values, standards, personality traits, and psychological routines. At what point did you begin to see my 'harmless flirting' as 'disrespect'? How much outside sex does it take before it's labeled excessive? Why are you so jealous/insecure/out of control/uptight/insensitive? In most cases, awareness, empathy, legitimization and creative accommodation can bridge the gap, but it's not always easy getting there.

We had very different personalities and very different perspectives on what was appropriate. We tried using rules, but they never seemed sufficient. One of us would get hurt or uncomfortable and we would have long talks and then we would conscientiously revise the rules. But it was more like we were negotiating - our focus was on right and wrong and fairness and compliance.

The breakthrough came when we finally stepped back and seriously considered what we each wanted and needed from the other. Instead of trying to change each other, we created new 'rules' that actually differed for the two of us. Our friends thought we were crazy, but the new rules allowed us both to get our different needs met. Instead of focusing on complying, we realized we actually wanted to honor and support each other's values and needs. I don't know why it took us so long to get there, but things became much easier when we started acting like we were on the same team... It was a few years after that we had this crazy idea that 'somebody' ought to do a study.

So, where's the support?

Most research shows that approximately two-thirds of long-term male couples who have been together for five years or more are honestly non-monogamous (Shernoff, LCSW, 2007). This means a majority of long-term male couples are creating their own unique models – despite societal injunctions. This is remarkable. And it makes us wonder why there isn't more overt support from the gay community. Why is there a reluctance to discuss non-monogamy – particularly in a community that believes in path-finding?

Although some study couples were very transparent about the openness of their relationship, this was not the case for most. As one participant shares:

Having an open relationship feels like a funny way of being in the closet again. Family and friends expect that we're monogamous, and we don't tell them we're not. It's like a secret. When we travel for work or to see family, we leave friends (and colleagues) at 10 pm and then we go out. In our community and society, it feels like something huge isn't being talked about or studied or understood.

When we began telling our friends, colleagues and family about this study, it did remind us of 'coming out'. It sometimes triggered dead silences or a polite change of subject. And it sometimes provoked deep, meaningful conversations.

As a community, we know from our own experiences of coming out that visibility and dialogue are critical. If you're bucking societal norms, it helps to have like-minded souls to reassure you that you're not alone. If you're charting a path where there is no road map, it helps to have folks who have been there or who can engage with you in your navigating. The study couples who reported having mentors were uniformly grateful.

Prior to initiating this study we encountered our own reluctance to publicly address this issue; we worried that talking about non-monogamy would be seen as jeopardizing the push for gay marriage. In the 4 years we've taken to complete the study, we never once encountered resistance from any group or organization. Perhaps this was a result of flying under the radar, but it also points to our own internalized fears of speaking about a taboo subject.

Ironically, when California legalized gay marriage (however briefly), we began hearing more and more of our study participants mention their marriages. This wasn't something we tracked, but a majority of the study couples from that point forward spoke of being married. Clearly they weren't equating marriage with monogamy! So, as a gay community, if we don't want to replicate the heterosexual divorce rate, we might begin looking for ways to talk more openly about how our relationships really work.

We hope this study opens the door to more candid discussions of responsible non-monogamous relationships. We strongly encourage others to research this topic to more thoroughly document:

- the wide range of behavior and choices being made
- the diversity of approach due to race, ethnicity, class and geography
- the generational perspectives
- the respective values of both monogamous and non-monogamous relationships.

In Conclusion

We think this study illustrates and validates the experience many male couples are having. It will be important to ascertain to what degree this kind of information is useful to non-monogamous couples, to couples considering non-monogamy, and to the larger community.

We'd like to end with our appreciation. Many, many thanks to the 86 couples who gave their time and perspective to this study!

— Blake Spears & Lanz Lowen
www.thecouplesstudy.com

About the Authors

Lanz Lowen, MS, MA

Lanz Lowen coaches executive leaders and facilitates teams in clarifying purpose, defining strategic priorities, resolving conflict, and increasing influence. Coaching engagements, as well as team interventions, typically begin with survey assessments and/or individual interviews.

Lanz is an adjunct staff-member at Stanford University's School of Business and at JFK University's Coaching Certificate Program. Prior to establishing his consulting practice, Lanz was the Manager of Organization Development and Training in the corporate offices of Mervyn's Department Stores.

Lanz Lowen has an M.S. in Industrial and Organizational Psychology from San Francisco State and an M.A. in Clinical Psychology from the Professional School of Psychology in San Francisco.

Other Interests:

Lanz was very involved in the early AIDS movement, running volunteer support groups for the AIDS Health Project and creating an independent video profiling long-term survivors (Living Courageously). He is a founding Board Member of Shamanic Circles, an occasional DJ and a dedicated flagger.

Blake Spears, MBA

Blake Spears is a founder and principal of InSight Healthcare and has eighteen years of experience in working with clients in the healthcare industry. Blake conducts research to assess market potential and the positioning of new pharmaceutical products and medical devices in a variety of clinical areas.

Blake has moderated over 150 focus groups and conducted thousands of in-depth interviews with clinicians and opinion leaders. Blake's academic credentials include a B.S. in chemical engineering from Virginia Polytechnic Institute and an MBA from the Stanford Graduate School of Business.

Other Interests:

Blake has been on the Board of Maitri Compassionate Care since 2001. Prior to that he served on the Board of the Golden Gate YMCA. He is a founding member of the Lesbian & Gay Student and Almuni Association of the Stanford Business School. Blake's interests include mediation, yoga, Tai Chi, and flagging.

For more information, visit www.thecouplesstudy.com

Made in the USA
Lexington, KY
24 October 2013